D0778724

DISCARDED

Imperialism: The Permanent Stage of Capitalism

Herb Addo

 The United Nations University

Volume 1 of *A World-System Critique of Eurocentric Conceptions in Political Economy*

Herb Addo is Senior Research Fellow at the Institute of International Relations, University of the West Indies, St. Augustine, Trinidad and Tobago

The United Nations University's Project on Goals, Processes, and Indicators of Development (GPID), 1978–1982, was initiated in response to widespread dissatisfaction with the prevailing concepts, theories, and strategies of development, which, three decades after the Second World War, had not fulfilled the expectations generated by them in the third world, and whose material achievements in the industrialized countries had come to be perceived by an increasing number of people as being fraught with ambiguity as well as being counter-developmental in their long-run tendencies. Taking up the development *problématique* on a global scale and maintaining that underdevelopment in the South and (over)development in the North were dialectically linked in the same global process of *mal*development, the Project concerned itself with a fundamental rethinking of the concepts of development, articulating the goals that should and could be pursued, the trends and counter-trends characterizing contemporary development processes, and alternative indicator systems for assessing and monitoring the dynamics of development. The books that have come out of the Project cover a broad spectrum of topics, ranging from theoretical reconsiderations, such as the present volume, to empirical analyses of ongoing developmental trends and transformational possibilities.

The United Nations University
Toho Seimei Building, 15–1 Shibuya 2-chome, Shibuya-ku, Tokyo 150, Japan
Tel.: (03) 499–2811   Telex: J25442   Cable: UNATUNIV TOKYO

Printed in Japan

HSDB-13/UNUP-484
ISBN 92-808-0484-7
United Nations Sales No. E.86.III.A.1
01500 C

Dedication

Never do those who have had exile thrust upon
them refer to the forests that saved them as small;
endearingly *little* perhaps, but never *small*.

To dear Lily and precious Kimo; to hospitable *little*
Trinidad and Tobago.

Contents

Part 3 A World-System Basis for a Theory of Imperialism

Part 4 Challenges and Responses

Acknowledgements

This book is a product of the Structural Interpretation of International Inequality Project (S3IP), launched in the mid-1970s in response to the existential disappointments which were then beginning to be experienced in the practice of development policies. I must acknowledge, however, that the full development of the S3IP occurred between 1978 and 1982 under the auspices of the United Nations University's research project on Goals, Processes, and Indicators of Development (UNU-GPID). The S3IP was fully incorporated into the Expansion-Exploitation/ Autonomy-Liberation Processes Sub-project of the GPID.

All the chapters in this book have been greatly influenced by critical discussions within the GPID.

The original essay from which this book developed, "The Continuity of Imperialism Thesis," was presented at the GPID meeting held in Geneva, October 1978. The draft manuscript of this book was presented and discussed in its entirety at the GPID Expansion-Exploitation Sub-group meeting held at the Max-Planck-Institut zur Erforschung der Lebensbedingungen der wissenschaftlich-technischen Welt, Starnberg, Federal Republic of Germany, March 1979. At a similar meeting in Trinidad, January 1981, a revised and final version of the manuscript, including many additional chapters, was presented and debated at length. It was at this latter meeting in Trinidad that the decision was taken to limit the scope of this book and to follow it with a second volume, addressing, in much greater detail and in much broader contexts, the implications of some of the arguments presented here. Chapter eight is a faithful reproduction of the discussion and the exchanges that took place at the Port of Spain meeting.

This book, therefore, not only owes a great debt to the GPID, it must be considered one of its products.

I thank the United Nations University for making real co-operation on an international scale possible, through the agency of the GPID. It was, indeed, a novel experiment. To my mind, the experiment was successful. The participatory experience was exhilarating. It helped to educate me in many ways and to socialize me into a world-wide system of interconnected, even interdependent, thoughts.

I am greatly indebted to all my friends and collaborators, both within and outside the GPID network, who made this book possible. Especially, I am grateful to the many who took particular interest in the development of the arguments. I must single out for mention here Samir Amin, George Aseniero, Neville Duncan, Locksley Edmondson, Johan Galtung, Anslem Francis, Andre Gunder Frank, Folker Fröbel, Jürgen Heinrichs, Terence Hopkins, Basil Ince, Tony Judge, Otto Kreye, Ramesh Ramsaran, Ato Sekyi-Otu, Immanuel Wallerstein, and Ralston Walters.

And, of course, I am grateful to the Institute of International Relations, University of the West Indies, St. Augustine, Trinidad and Tobago, for making it possible for me to exchange ideas and arguments on the subject with my students since 1975. I thank Jeanne Callender for her speedy typing of the earlier drafts of this book and my colleague, Dr. Paula Mark, for her many editorial suggestions.

In particular, I am indebted to Lily Addo for her research and secretarial support in the S3IP since its inception.

Needless to say, I alone am responsible for any errors of judgement, misconceptions, inaccuracies, and inadequacies in this book. However, I insist that responsibility for correcting these errors cannot be mine alone. In these matters, as Walter Rodney once put it, responsibility is collective. Martin Carter, the Guyanese poet, says it even better: "All ah we is involved."

St. Augustine, Trinidad and Tobago
October 1985

H.A.

Prologue

The decades of the 1960s and the 1970s were pre-eminently a period which brought to the surface an acute sense of the urgent need to confront the great disorder that surrounded the actualization of the idea of development. A new level of consciousness was reached during this period, and it led to many international conferences and meetings, the various resolutions, calls, demands, and even action programmes that were intended to bring some progressive order and rational reasoning to bear on the management of human affairs as they pertained to the realization of the idea of development.

The active fronts of this rising consciousness were many; but each front experienced deep disappointment and frustration. By the mid-1970s, we had come to the crucial realization that the conception of development as the pragmatic and incremental bridging of the "North-South gap," through diffusionist policies and imitative strategies, might not only be an unworkable proposition but possibly an undesirable one as well. This led to the pressing need to search for new intellectual bases from which to approach the dissolution or the negation of underdevelopment.

This, in turn, necessitated the need to provide the historical grounds from which to proceed to identify those processes, both subtle and overt, which sustain underdevelopment as well as the need to demonstrate how the very negation of these processes would amount to true development: associative humanizing cultures of production and appropriation to meet basic human needs for all equitably.

The construction of such bases is by no means easy, but, like the proverbial journey of a thousand miles, it must begin with a first step: the clarification of the many concepts, the interrelatedness of which explains the development *problématique*. These conceptual clarifications must be informed by a sense of history. They must be informed by the rising consciousness brought about by new evaluations of what we have in the

1

world and what we have come to appreciate differently about the
dynamics of world-history in evolution.

Towards this awesome goal, Immanuel Wallerstein has succinctly pointed
to the reasons why the first step should be conceptual clarification. He
wrote that:

> The important thing for living men, and for scholars and scientists as
> their collective intellectual expression, is to situate the options
> available in the contemporary situation in terms of the patterns we can
> discern in the historical past. In this task, conceptual clarification is the
> most constant need, and as life goes on and new experiences occur, we
> learn, if we are wise, to reject and reformulate the partial truths of our
> predecessors, and to unmask the ideological obscurantism of the
> self-interested upholders of encrusted privilege.[1]

In this book, I use the term "Eurocentricity" to describe the prevailing
"ideological obscurantism." It is meant to describe the heavy dominance,
that is, the "encrusted privilege," of European culture in the evolution of
the modern world-system, both in the realms of fact and ideas. By
Europe, I am referring to the European culture as it exists in Europe
proper and as it predominates in Europe of the Diaspora — the United
States, Canada, Australia, New Zealand, and South Africa. I use the term
Europe rather than Western Europe or any other comparable term
because I want to stress the cultural dominance in the modern
world-system and its implied economic, political, and other forms of
domination.

It matters very little whether there is agreement on the exact year in
which the modern world-system emerged, so long as there is agreement
that it occurred some time in the late fifteenth century. I am partial to
Eric Williams' view that the "year" 1415–1492, marked by Vasco Da
Gama's and Christopher Columbus' exploration triumphs,[2] is as good as
any year in the fifteenth century for dating the origin of the modern
world-system. Thus, for contextual clarity, I use the expressions "in the
fifteenth century" or "in the late fifteenth century." Also, I refer to the
historical duration since that time as *world-history* in order to distinguish
this most relevant period from the unspecific and the imprecise term
history of the world.

I employ my understanding of the world-system methodology to argue
that, in order to understand the development *problématique*, thinking on

the matter must be de-Eurocentrized for it to have any meaning at all. This is to say that it is only in terms of the historical evolution and the continuing dynamics of the world-system as a *whole*, from its very inception to the present, that the development-underdevelopment dialectic can be grasped fully.

Consequently, it is only through a full confrontation with the logic and dynamics of the world-system that authentic and realistic alternative aims, perspectives, and strategies can begin to be conceived. Hence, the description of this book and its intended sequel as "A World-System Critique of Eurocentric Conceptions in Political Economy."

The main thrust of the critique is that the three main perspectives in political economy, the liberal, radical, and Marxist, apparent differences notwithstanding, have in common some fundamental Eurocentric properties that blind us to other (real) meanings of our world-history. The Eurocentric world-view does not encourage other "valid" interpretations of world-history, and yet, because of its dominance, it is impossible to attempt other interpretations without discussing Eurocentricity.

Our perspective is intended for us to begin to suspect that perhaps there is nothing innocent about Eurocentric epistemology/methodology: that perhaps liberalism is not the gentlemanly ideology it pretends to be and that Marxism may not be the height of creative thinking, as its adherents claim it to be.

I should state that this book does not claim to do more than suggest that if we examined our basic concepts and categories in political economy, we would find that they are as Eurocentric as they can only be expected to be, given the Eurocentric dominance in our given world.

Having in mind the promise of a detailed and broader discussion in its sequel, this book pretends to do no more than illustrate the highly probable validity of the Eurocentric charge with its treatment of imperialism. To the point, I regard the views in this book as composing an elaborate working hypothesis, helpful in elucidating certain obscurities in the links between the specificities of capitalist expansion, domination, and exploitation as they pertain to the theory of (under)development. The hope is that this book can help in uncovering certain theoretically unconnected insights. I approach the views in this book in the spirit that they are all open to correction and that they are to be discarded if and whenever they do not facilitate the progress of the theory of development.

Finally, I should say that the nature of the subject makes it impossible to completely avoid the semblance of polemics. I only hope that I have kept polemics to the minimum and, for that matter, in their appropriate place. Presentational clarity demanded that in parts of the book I be deliberate, dry, and even uninteresting; and if I have not been fluent all the way through, it is for the reason that repetition is not totally avoidable.

Notes

1. Immanuel Wallerstein, "Dependence in an Inter-dependent World: The Limited Possibilities of Transformation within the Capitalist World Economy," in Heraldo Muñoz, ed., *From Dependency to Development: Strategies to Overcome Underdevelopment and Inequality* (Westview Press, Boulder, Col., 1981; reprinted from *African Studies Review* 18, no. 1 [1974]: 1–26), p. 268.
2. Eric Williams, *From Columbus to Castro: The History of the Caribbean 1492–1969* (Andre Deutsch, London, 1978), pp. 13–17.

Part One

The Problem

Chapter One

Introduction

This book turns on the strong conviction that a newly synthesized
formulation of the concept imperialism is urgently needed to understand
the persistence of underdevelopment or the development of peripheral
capitalism; and that this can be done most conveniently outside the strict
confines of Eurocentricity.

The underlying belief is that in showing how this concept can be
understood outside Eurocentric sympathies, we can gain a much better
understanding of the structural relationals and the sustaining processes
that explain the world not only to Europe but to the whole world. The
conviction is that the refinement of this concept leads not only to other
concept refinements but shows how such refinements can combine to
betray hidden relationships which can be of great importance in
understanding how our present world, as a whole, came to be what it is
and what constitutes its transformational potential. Indeed, if concepts
are really refined to reflect the world reality problem, the global
problématique, properly, they can lead to refined analyses of historical
developments in terms of their *goals, processes,* and *indicators.*

If, therefore, we attempt here to show how the concept imperialism
should be understood in order to explain the *entire* world to the entire
world, it is because of the initial insistence that the non-European parts
of the world have always been participants in the unfolding of
world-history, from its very inception, and not just helpless objects, who
do no more than look on as history passes them by.

The book begins with a discussion of the methodological contrast
between Eurocentric properties and world-system postulates. The
discussion is cast in the contending mode that the world-system approach
allows for the full recognition of the participation of third world societies
in the unfolding of world-history both as object and subject. That is, this
way of looking at world-history allows for the recognition of the inputs

of third world societies into the causes why the historical past has produced the historical present, with respect to the prominent feature of the development-underdevelopment dialectic.

These two recognitions allow for a crucial admission: that periphery sources contribute to the persistence of imperialism. Third world societies are, therefore, not necessarily and potentially as impotent in providing appropriate inputs into the transformational requirements of the world-system as Eurocentric epistemology and conventional wisdom would have us believe.

From this methodological mode we construct a critical scheme, the foundations of which derive from insight drawn from a particular reading of the logic of the world-system methodology. The scheme allows for the critical appreciation of Eurocentric renditions of imperialism according to the *imprecise* and the *over-precise* endowments of historical concepts in Eurocentric historiography; and it is made up of a composite historic logic, which argues that the logic of the world-system in evolution embraces the dialectically interrelating logics of all its subparts. Each part of the world-system, then, is to be understood first and foremost as the product of world-history: a product of all that it has encountered, both as an object and as a subject, in the unfolding of world-history.

The critical scheme is applied to the liberal, radical, and Marxist conceptions of imperialism in three succeeding chapters. This is done for two main reasons. First, to show that all these conceptions are Eurocentric at their epistemological base. Second, to show that, sheared of their Eurocentric character, these three conceptions of imperialism can contribute, even if negatively, to the new formulation that we are after.

In chapter three, I argue that the liberal conception of imperialism, because of its imprecision, is *transhistoric* and *transepochal*. It is too fluid in nature and, therefore, for my purposes, too elastic to be historico-analytically useful.

The radical conception of imperialism is treated in chapter four. I present it as a rigid conception which violates the strict sensitivity needed to respect the historic specificity of world-history in its totality.

The Marxist conception of imperialism is no less rigid. In chapter five, I argue that this conception of imperialism, because of its over-precise nature, is too blunt to be analytically useful in the study of world-history from the peripheral perspective.

Chapters three, four, and five have a common structure. All these chapters begin with a close textual analysis of the main works that serve as the intellectual sources for the different conceptions of imperialism. I then proceed to criticize these conceptions from the point of view of the critical scheme. These sources, however, are not too clear in all cases.

I use Schumpeter's works as the intellectual source for the liberal conception of imperialism because of his immense influence on liberal thinking on the subject, which, many will agree, is due to Schumpeter's ability to write elegantly while communicating complex ideas in very clear and simple ways.

Many radicals consider Hobson's works on the subject early this century as the starting point, even though the sources of his ideas on the subject can be traced back to other writings.[1] Hobson's claim to fame rests on his journalistic Manichaean excesses in seeing imperialism principally in terms of negative social and economic calculations, and on the false appearances that he was sympathetic to the imperialized races.

The Marxist intellectual source is attributed to Lenin's work, even though other Marxists had expressed themselves earlier on the subject. It is Lenin's dominating and magnetic revolutionary personality as well as the forceful clarity of his writing which account for his works on the subject being universally accepted as the Marxist intellectual source of origin.

In chapter six, entitled "The Thesis," I undertake to show how, according to my understanding of the subject, we may proceed to view imperialism in its historically precise conception, if we are to avoid Eurocentric pitfalls. It is in this chapter that I present *the continuity of imperialism thesis* in its structural form and in its phase-relationship with capitalism.

The *thesis* is that the imperialism we associate with capitalism is *sui generis*; and that it has been an abiding attribute of capitalism since its nascence in Europe in the late fifteenth century. The argument is that it is only the forms of imperialism that have changed with the development of world capitalism; but that its historical vocation of facilitating the leakage of capital from the periphery to the centre of the world-system has remained intact.

Chapter seven is where the attempt is made to clarify what the identity of the thesis is and to point to some indicative hypotheses that can be derived from it. In addition, I try to anticipate some questions on, and criticisms of, the *thesis*.

It became clear to me during several exchanges that if the reality problem I was concerned with was the continuity or the persistence of imperialism all through the history of world capitalism, then I had to approach it in two stages. First, I had to establish the continuity of imperialism as a fact all through capitalist historicity. This is what I try to do in this book, volume 1. Second, I had to proceed to ask and examine, in great detail, why this must be so, that is, why imperialism must be continuously persistent in the history of capitalism and why it must be natural and therefore in no way unusual to capitalism. This is precisely what I shall attempt to do in volume 2, tentatively titled *On the Persistence of Peripheral Capitalism: Who Participates in Underdeveloping Whom, How, and Why?*

As I have already stated, chapter eight is the proceedings of the last in-house GPID discussion of the final version of the manuscript. It is included here because it is believed that it could be useful for readers as a built-in review of the book itself.

In the epilogue, chapter nine, I provide a more considered reflection on the overall meaning of the criticisms advanced in anticipation of what would be required in volume 2. For example, reflection suggested that the Eurocentric indictment must be prosecuted much more fundamentally, much more vigorously, far beyond the mere identification of Eurocentric properties in contrast with world-system postulates, as initially important as this identification is. It also became clear that I should treat in greater detail what it is that I mean by capitalist historicity; and also that there was the need to cast the centre-periphery relational underpinnings of peripheral capitalism in terms of a dialectical unity, rather than in terms of mere unequal interdependence.

In anticipation of objections to the use of the term imperialism to describe the evolution of capitalist exploitation on its march towards maximum world scale since the late fifteenth century, let me say that surely another term could have been chosen to represent this phenomenon. But why should we choose a new term, when one already exists that covers the essentials of what we are dealing with? It would have remained a puzzle why imperialism was used to describe everything else but what we describe here, were it not that our world-system discussion of Eurocentricity provides a key to the puzzle. The main things wrong with the usages of the term have been the unlimited historical specificity with which liberals endow the term and the extremely limited historical specificity which radicals and Marxists impose on it. With the proper historical specificity introduced, it seems superfluous to invent any other term to represent our position. We would definitely have had to choose another term to stand for what we describe, were it not that the specificity of the historical ensemble which we seek to identify and capture, for contemporary usage, can be contained most adequately by the term imperialism, as we define, interpret, and use it in this book.

I say this fully aware of Fritz Machlup's position that "priority in the use of a novel meaning of a term is no cause for pride; in fact it betrays a lack of 'terminological discipline' and a want of linguistic inventiveness — for when a writer creates or modifies a concept he ought also to coin a new word to denote it, rather than corrupt the language and spread confusion."[2]

This admonition is appropriate where the priority in such use is being done in a given epistemological context. But where there is a departure in epistemological basis, priority in the use of a novel meaning of a term may be a cause for pride. The reasons and the justification for the pride are to be deduced from the nature of the epistemological departure. The world-system methodology, as we understand it and hope to demonstrate in the body of the work, provides a clear basis for departure from the Eurocentric epistemology in political economy; and, therefore, it is entitled to have its own novel meanings of key terms. Imperialism is one such term.[3]

Notes

1. For a demonstration of this matter, see Eric Williams' treatment of Adam Smith, as a historian, and the Duke of New Castle of 1895, who had anticipated Hobson on aspects of anti-socio-economics of slavery and imperialism. Refer to Eric Williams, *British Historians and the West Indies* (Andre Deutsch, London, 1966), especially pp. 89 and 95.
2. Fritz Machlup, *Essays on Economic Semantics* (Prentice-Hall, Englewood Cliffs, N.J., 1963), p. 12.
3. For a discussion of this controversy as it applies to the term "interdependence," see David A. Baldwin, "Interdependence and Power: A Conceptual Analysis," *International Organization* 34, no. 4 (1980): 471–506.

Chapter Two

Eurocentric Properties versus World-System Postulates

Eurocentric Properties

Ideally, any epistemology/methodology that claims to explain the historical unfolding of the world to the entire world should have a historiography which is informed by universally valid historical concepts. In our present world, the situation is far from ideal in this respect, in that there are many common concepts in social history that appear to be useful in serious analysis only in the limited sense of explaining matters of European concern to Europeans and Europeanized peoples.

Therefore, I begin from the initial conviction that by far most of the theories in political economy express Eurocentric views which, from the peripheral perspective, cloud rather than expose the reality problem of the capitalist world-system. The burden, then, is on me to point to the epistemological/methodological sources of this clouding and to suggest an alternative which can expose the reality problem of situating the periphery squarely in the mainstream of world-history.

By Eurocentric, I mean that the conventional usages of many concepts, including *capitalism, imperialism,* and *development,* and the interrelationships between them are bound too closely to European peculiarities and interests in the study of world-history. Specifically, I object to Eurocentric renditions of concepts for two principal reasons: the contents endowed the concepts; and the analytic and other purposes which their meanings and their uses serve in interpreting history, past, present, and future.

Eurocentrics tend to believe that the non-European world is merely underdeveloped Europe; and they tend to believe that, given time, non-Europeans will come to understand Eurocentric concepts just as Europeans do. But then, this twin belief serves the much larger belief that Europe, in the sense we have described it in the prologue, is larger than, or at least as large as, the world. This larger belief does not merely imply, it means that the world matters only because Europe is in it. In general terms, it means that non-European areas of the world are considered as no more than an arena for the secondary expressions of the European ethos and pathos in the unfolding of world-history.

The Eurocentric charge, therefore, expresses the view that the meanings and the usages of many common concepts in political economy make historical and analytic sense only in the peculiar and dominating European circumstances within world-history, but none whatsoever in the subordinated circumstances of the non-European parts of the world. If, in their Eurocentric forms, these concepts explain Europe to the world and the world to Europe, then the argument is that they are not equipped to explain the world to the world. They simply cannot explain the world to non-European areas, in the vital terms of confronting European domination with their subordination, for the purpose of transforming the capitalist world-system.

If the idea is to explain the world in evolution to the world as it is, and if the fact of the matter is that Europe matters only because it is part of the world and not because it is in any sense larger than the world, then we must take the Eurocentric charge seriously. We cannot take its validity for granted. It must be demonstrated through showing *how* certain crucial, even if common, concepts and their usages bear the Eurocentric imprint.

In addition to the general Eurocentric propensities mentioned above, there are certain other properties which appear to characterize the Eurocentric approach to the historiography of the modern world. It seems to be a basic requirement that Eurocentric approaches to modern history should gloss over the extremely vital difference between the initiation and the unfolding of the history of our one world, *world-history*, a "world-wide" related matter since the late fifteenth century, and the *history of the world* before this period, a set of non-interdependent localized feudalisms.[1] Eurocentric views of modern history tend to gloss over this major difference principally because they tend to mistake the European dominance and initiatives in world-history for world-history itself. For this reason, the Eurocentric perspective tends to view world-history with strict reference to the *consistencies* and *inconsistencies*, the *continuities* and the *discontinuities*, and the *constancies* and the *inconstancies* of the European scene and the European memory.

Eurocentric interpretations of world-history draw world-historical specificities around variations that are immediately meaningful only in European circumstances. For this reason, any variations or constancies, which world-history as such may have, tend to be lost in European-specific particularities and peculiarities. The result tends to be that world-historical contexts and their specifics end up being either *imprecise* or *over-precise*.

By imprecise, I mean that such concepts are endowed with meanings that are too broad because they are not *historically specific* enough to respect the *historic identity* of the world capitalist system. By over-precise, I refer to the extreme specificity that restricts the *historic space* concepts must have if they are to respect the proper identity of capitalist historicity.

Many concepts can illustrate this charge very well. No single world-historical concept, however, has suffered in the hands of Eurocentrics as much as the concept imperialism. Certainly, no single concept illustrates the Eurocentric charge better.

The *imprecise* and the *over-precise* conceptions of imperialism violate the concept's analytic precision, which should be derived from the historic specificity of the modern world-system if the concept imperialism is to be of any use in interpreting history in such a way that it can help explain the multiple presents for the purpose of influencing the multiple futures.

The thesis of this book is that the imperialism of the modern world-system differs so much in theme and motive from earlier kindred phenomena that if we use the concept to describe the expansionist and exploitative facts of capitalism in evolution, then we should not use the same term to describe the expansionist and exploitative impulses in earlier economic forms, because they had different historic themes and motives. Closely linked to this position is the argument that imperialism is itself a process that derives its dynamism and changing forms from the development of capitalism, which has always been "world scale." The connection between imperialism and world capitalism is so close, imperialism is so much an intimate part of world capitalism that capitalism cannot exist without imperialism. We may in fact see the two phenomena as synonymous.

Eurocentric sympathies lead to dogmatic and unjustifiable interference with the proper historical specificity, which the concept imperialism needs for it to have any meaning at all for world-system analytic purposes. The historical *reason* which should suggest the specific period, within which imperialism should find its relevant meaning for contemporary usage, is made to appear as if it is to be found only in the histories of core European countries, in world-historical time. Thus, rather than the core economies being seen as part of a world-economy, they are seen as constituting the world-economy. And rather than seeing the peripheral economies as part of the world-economy, they are seen as unimportant arenas for the secondary expressions of the core countries' economies. The Eurocentric view of world-history leaves the strong impression that underlying it all is a silent conspiracy to recognize neither the *participation* of the peripheral economies in the world-economy and its history, nor their *contribution* to this essentially expansive, polarizing and, therefore, unjust economy in its relentless pursuit of its historic theme, which is the accumulation of capital in the centre and away from the periphery.

The modern European economy and its history have unquestionably dominated the modern world-economy and its history. It is not Eurocentric to recognize this fact. But since the European identity is also unquestionably and deeply influenced by the world-economy, it becomes Eurocentric when, in reading world-history, relevant concepts are endowed with meanings which are comfortable to use only in their strictly European contexts. It becomes Eurocentric when concepts, which belong to the world-wide and the unitary contexts of the world-system and its history, are used as though they stand for something that Europe, in its isolation from the rest of the unfolding world, did to the rest of the world in a series of unconnected one-shot acts, rather than as something that Europe and the rest of the world, in interacting over the common course of modern history, did to affect the modern world-system as we know it.

The reading of world-history becomes extremely Eurocentric when world-historical concepts are understood, not in relation to the singular axis of the series of differences and similarities that characterize the development of the modern world-economy, but as though they describe the variations and discontinuities of European history alone. It becomes painfully Eurocentric when the changing central tones of the European economy are made to obscure those of the world-economy. As a result, Eurocentric epochs and phases are made to overshadow constancies, continuities, and the subtle flow of variations at the world-system level. This may be bad enough, but there is worse. Eurocentrics, in treating European history as though it were world-history itself, do not treat, in fact, European history at all. What they treat are the histories of the

European hegemonic powers. Thus, what we have in the end is a series of hegemony-centred histories masquerading as world-history.[2]

The charge that existing conceptions of imperialism are Eurocentric exists in the literature, but it is far from being a prominent theme. It is mentioned only here and there. And there are even faint suggestions that if it is properly understood, within the confines of certain Eurocentric theories, the concept's specific historical context could span a part of the history of the modern world-economy, if not all of it.[3] However, so strong is the Eurocentric grip on the theories of imperialism that no more than a brief mention need be made to point out the small stature of this charge in the literature.

Gallagher and Robinson point to the extremely limited but insightful criticism that the proper period for imperialism, in the case of Britain, the hegemonic power of the time, was not the late nineteenth century but all through that century, because British policy did not change much during the period.[4] In this regard, they point to the more important insight that the imperialist events in Africa during the late nineteenth century had their roots both in Europe and in Africa. This indicates that Africa and other non-European areas played roles in the unfolding of world-history.

The majority of the essays in *Studies of the Theory of Imperialism* give the impression that the Eurocentric charge does not exist, in that they see imperialism as a late nineteenth century phenomenon.[5] Where the essays by Thomas Hodgkin and Ronald Robinson touch on the Eurocentric charge, Roger Owen's discussion of them in the introduction suggests that they made a strong impression. However, Sutcliffe's views on the matter, in the conclusion of that book, suggest that only an "orthodox" re-reading of the Marxist theory of imperialism is required to refute the Eurocentric charge, as presented by these two writers.[6]

Even though, in the above book of essays on imperialism, Robinson continues to see imperialism as only a nineteenth century phenomenon, he calls attention to the important point that the imperialism of this period was not possible without the "collaborative mechanisms" in the imperialized territories — the bridgeheads needed for effective domination.[7]

By far the clearest exposition to date, of the charge that prevailing conceptions of imperialism are Eurocentric, is contained in Hodgkin's essay, "Some African and Third World Theories of Imperialism."[8] He expresses the view that theories of imperialism available in the West are Eurocentric because "they are by Europeans and, very largely they are about the economies, societies, the political systems of European states."[9] Hodgkin prosecutes the charge admirably by calling attention to the contributions which non-European writers can make towards the construction of a general theory of imperialism. He reviews the works of many non-European writers on imperialism to suggest that their contributions can alert a general theory of imperialism to the social consequences of imperialism for both the colonizers and the colonized.[10]

Hodgkin states that a theory of imperialism should seek to explain the following questions, among others: How did there come into being the particular kinds of relationships of domination and subjection between "Westerners" and "non-Westerners"? In what respects does modern Western imperialism differ from other empire-building processes in other kinds of historical situations?[11] The first question must be asked, except that it must be understood to imply *why* this particular domination-subjection relationship came about and *when* it was initiated. The second question which Hodgkin raises is, of course, the locus of the much-needed historical specificity, if the concept is to make sense for our contemporary circumstances within the capitalist historicity.

Another crucial question which Hodgkin tries to answer, through his review of non-European theories of imperialism, is whether there has ever, in fact, been an "epoch of imperialism," in any intelligible sense of the term. His answer is that, indeed, there was such a period. He writes: "The theories of the [non-Europeans] ... particularly those who lived through and experienced the phase of maximum imperialism (post-1870s), seem never to have seriously doubted the existence of a reality corresponding with the idea."[12]

In the light of the above, it becomes extremely important to state that the argument that imperialism has been continuous throughout the capitalist historicity does not reject nor contest the position that the post-1870s experience *differed* in intensity and in form from the earlier experiences within the capitalist historicity. What is to be contested, in fact rejected, is the view that the two experiences differ in historic theme, motive, and intent and, therefore, that the "old" and the "new" imperialisms are qualitatively different historic(al) phenomena; and further that, for this reason, the two experiences are totally distinct in terms of their spatio-temporal referents. What is to be denied is that the so-called "epoch of imperialism" was something which is not connected with —

that is, it was not produced or even aided by — the so-called old imperialism; and what is to be rejected is the slightest hint that earlier domination-subjection experiences (in Euro-American, Euro-African, Euro-Asian, and Euro-Oceanic relations) during the mercantilist period of capital accumulation differ so much that, even with hindsight, they cannot be understood as being connected with the post-1870 experiences all over the world, within the global "plan" of capitalist development. The suggestion here is that all the diverse experiences referred to, and the differences between them in spatio-temporal terms, can be adequately contained by the concept imperialism, understood, at the first encounter, to mean no more and no less than the exploitative aspects of the world-wide expansionist processes making up the global development of the capitalist world-economy and leading to the pauperization of some parts of the world and the enrichment of other parts.[13]

Broadly, my point of departure is the argument that imperialism has developed together with the development of capitalism from its very beginning and that it has been "world-wide" from the very beginning of the world-system. Exactly my point of departure is the distinction I refuse to make between the so-called *old* and *new* imperialisms within the historicity of capitalism. This distinction, which I do not respect, originates from the exaggerated Eurocentric distinction between the so-called "primitive accumulation" and capitalist accumulation. I argue that, from the world-system perspective, imperialism has been an accompanying phenomenon of capitalism and that what is important in this respect is the *essential continuity* of the phenomenon which derives from the *essential continuity of the capitalist historic theme* of accumulating capital in the centre of the world-system and away from the periphery since the late fifteenth century, and not the *changing forms* which the imperialist phenomenon takes as world capitalism changes its own forms to facilitate its theme. This position is what I refer to as *the continuity of imperialism thesis.*

It is for these reasons that the following statement by Hodgkin is both clarificatory and supportive of the *thesis*:

[The non-European] theories were, however, perfectly well aware of the *aspect of continuity as well as change*. They perceived, and indeed emphasized, *the historical connections between the older forms of Western dominance, ascendancy, influence, pressure, exploitation, etc. combined with limited annexation, and the new model of imperialism*, of which the typical expression, so far as Africa was concerned, *was the*

18

establishment of organized colonial systems. The "epoch of imperialism," they argued, *must be understood as simply the most recent phase in the whole prolonged historical process by which the European nations used superior technological and military power to enslave and subjugate non-European peoples for [European peoples'] enrichment.* They were particularly concerned *to stress the resemblances between the underlying assumptions of modern imperialism and of the European slave trade....*[14]

Hodgkin came to this succint statement of the essentials of the *thesis* indirectly by way of reviewing the works of non-European theorists, whom he calls "consumer theorists." I intend, in the following chapters, to press further the Eurocentric charge in order to strengthen the *thesis*. However, unlike Hodgkin, I shall do this directly by reviewing European or "producer" theories of imperialism. I intend to show that Eurocentric interpretations of imperialism are no more than apologia of Eurocentric apologetics, all along the ideological continuum, for the state of our contemporary world.

World-System Postulates

In referring to the three abstract conditions of Marx's theory of the capitalist mode of production, namely the three generalizations of commodity form of products, commodity form of labour power, and competition between capitals, Amin says:

> These conditions *did not fall from the heaven* of imagination: they express in abstract terms the reality of the capitalist mode of production, which Marx studied and of which mid-nineteenth-century England provided the concrete model. *The world capitalist system is another plane of reality, which also needs to be defined in abstract terms if it is to be analysed theoretically.* (Emphases added.)[15]

It can be inferred from Amin's words that we cannot do this without reference to the history of capitalism in its totality and at the world-system level. But then, as Amin argues, this can be done only after Marxists and others have shed their "West-centred outlook,"[16] which they can only do after they have realized and accepted that capitalism has been "world-wide" from its very beginning. When we take the above together with Amin's view that primitive accumulation is something permanent and contemporary[17] and consider all this in the context of his enhancing review of Wallerstein's *The Modern World-System*,[18] it becomes not merely clear but obvious that indeed the world-system should be accorded an identity of its own.

Once this is done, it should become difficult to turn a deaf ear to the implied message that to understand our contemporary capitalist world (its structural-relational or textual identity) properly, we need to understand its key problems and their roots of origin, within the context of the development of world-history as the process of accumulating capital on a world-scale, implying the draining of capital from the periphery to the centre of the world-economy.

Frank has made the process of capital accumulation his main subject of study for a long time now.[19] In his *World Accumulation, 1492–1789* he opens the chapter "Conclusions: On So-Called Primitive Accumulation," with the statement:

The process of capital accumulation is a, if not the, principal motor of modern history and constitutes the central problem examined in this book. Yet capital accumulation, and its treatment here, poses a number of fundamental theoretical and therefore also empirical questions that remain largely unresolved. These questions fall into four related categories: (1) primitive, primary, and capitalist capital accumulation; (2) the unequal structure and relations of production, circulation, and realization in capital accumulation; (3) uneven transformation of capital accumulation through stages, cycles, and crises; and (4) unending class struggle in capital accumulation, through the state, war, and revolution. Insofar as one single and continuous process of capital accumulation has existed in this world for several centuries, this heuristic division of the problem into unequal structure, uneven process, and so on is necessarily arbitrary. The structural inequality and temporal unevenness of capital accumulation, on the other hand, are inherent to capitalism.

A major open question concerns the basis and modalities of capitalist accumulation of capital itself, and particularly the transition to this process through "so-called primitive accumulation" — as well as the transition again from capital to "socialist accumulation." Insofar as I argue that during the past few centuries the world has experienced a single, all-embracing, albeit unequal and uneven, process of capital accumulation that has been capitalist for at least two centuries, it is necessary to inquire how this process began, on what bases it developed, and to what extent it has undergone important changes.[20]

When Frank says that one single and continuous process of capital accumulation has existed in this world for several centuries, I understand *several centuries* to mean since the sixteenth century, at least. I understand his *this world* to mean the distinction of world-history from the many "localized" histories prior to the initiation of the capitalist "world."

Under normal circumstances, under circumstances without Eurocentric excesses, Frank's statements would have served as the basis for the first encounter with the development of underdevelopment reality. But given the circumstances, the Eurocentric circumstances of our world, Frank, many years after dramatizing thought along these lines, still felt compelled to justify these statements to, and defend them from, orthodox Marxists and others by immaculate references to Marx's works.[21] This chapter on conclusions in his magistral work on world accumulation is practically devoted to such justification and defence.[22]

Wallerstein brings a totally different style to the prosecution of the Eurocentric charge. To be sure, this style is not exactly unmindful of Eurocentric Marxists; but it is a style offering, perhaps, the most confident point of departure for stating and situating the continuity of imperialism thesis.[23] His method hinges on the theoretical aspects of capitalist development which, though far from pleasing to Eurocentric Marxists, frees him from most of the misleading Eurocentric compulsions to erect partial historical truth into phoney not-to-be-impeached dogmas. Wallerstein's works in this regard do not blow Eurocentric "ideasyncracies"[24] into "ideologies" and parade them as universal explanatories. Rather, they provide the basis from which to explode such Eurocentric universal myths. Wallerstein's world-system methodology shares the common belief with Oliver Cox, Frank, and Amin that, in the analysis of social reality, history and theory are not only indispensable, but that indeed they are the same: "theory is history."[25]

Wallerstein begins his world-system methodology with the assumption that the unit of analysis is an economic entity, to be measured by the existence of effective division of labour, and that "the relationship of such economic boundaries to political cultural boundaries is variable, and therefore must be determined by empirical research for each historic case."[26] My interpretation of this variability is that it then immediately becomes the subject of *history* — history which should be understood and appreciated without compromise within the limits and the temper of the *historic* time. He explains:

Once we assume that the unit of analysis is ... a 'world-system' and not the 'state' or the 'nation' or the 'people', then much changes in the outcome of the analysis ... we shift from a concern with the attributive characteristics of states. We shift from seeing class ... as groups within a world-economy. And the debate of universalism vs. particularism as *alternative* modes of analysis becomes bypassed, since these terms reflect in fact a dialectical antinomy that pervades all social action.[27]

The only social system within the framework, the objectivity of which is the honesty of analysis within it,[28] is the *world-system* within which states, nations, or groups are to be seen only as kinds of organizational entities among others.[29] But what is this world-system and how does it differ from earlier and other systems which could claim to be "world"? On this, Wallerstein says:

In the late fifteenth and early sixteenth centuries, [i.e. during the long sixteenth century] there came into existence what we may call a European world-economy. It was not an empire yet it was as spacious as a grand empire and shared some features with it ... it was different, and new. It was a kind of social system the world has not really known before and which is the distinctive feature of the modern world-system. It is an economic but not a political entity, unlike empires, city-states and nation-states.... It is a 'world' system, not because it encompasses the whole world, but because it is larger than any juridicially-defined political unit. And it is a *'world-economy'* because the basic linkage between the parts of the system is economic, although this was reinforced to some extent by political arrangements and even confederal structures.[30]

Empires differ from this new world-system. Empires, as Wallerstein recalls Eisenstadt, have been around the world for some 5,000 years: they are, in fact, political or "primitive means of economic domination."[31] But what distinguishes this world-system from previous non-world-systems, such as empires? It is not *exploitation*. It is the *efficiency of* the *exploitation* of some (the many) by others (the few) along all the various levels within the world-system. While the strength of an empire lay in the fact that it guaranteed economic flow from the periphery to the centre by force and by monopolistic advantages in trade, its weakness lay in *cumbersome* and *inefficient* maintenance of it. Herein lies the main difference:

It is the social achievement of the modern world, ... to have invented
the technology that makes it possible to increase the flow of surplus
from the lower strata to the upper strata, from the periphery to the
centre, from the majority to the minority, by eliminating the 'waste'
of too cumbersome a political superstructure.[32]

The name of this world-system is capitalism, not because it was called
and known as such from the very beginning but because, from its
unsuspecting origins, it came to be known as such at about the middle of
its evolution to date.[33] The origins of capitalism are uncontroversially
European and it was born out of the "crises of feudalism" in Europe in
the "long sixteenth century." What is distinctly curious about capitalism
is its *origins* and the *real history of its evolution*; but, in our context, much
more curious is its *evolution*.

It may have originated in Europe, but its history has become the history
of the world, not the history of Europe alone. But why is this so? This
question can be answered, and attempts have been made to answer it by
different Eurocentric interpretations of the history of capitalism. For our
purposes, the answer is this: the real history of capitalism shows it to
have been expansive, not easily contained and confined. Its appetite
seems to have grown by what it fed on — the production for markets and
amassing of profits, to encourage more production for larger markets,
and more profits *ad infinitum*. This is not to say that all that it feeds on is
necessarily good for it, at any one time, or in the short term.[34] Certainly,
whatever it feeds on is not good for it in the final analysis.[35]

The capitalist mode of production has a total history, which can be
distinguished into "phases" or "stages" for analytic purposes only. But
when the concern with this history is its expansionary fact, then this
history is to be seen in its totality, not in its chopped-up portions.

The main lesson in Wallerstein's work is that capitalism is only feasible
within the framework of a world-economy, not within a world-empire, as
he distinguished between the two. As of 1450, the stage was set in
Europe, but not elsewhere, for the creation of this capitalist
world-economy, based on the two key institutions of world-wide division
of labour and of bureaucratic statism in the heart of this system. This
lesson may be forgotten with reference to *development* as the process of
prescribed or identified changes in world-history. However, what cannot
be forgotten, without meandering into marginalist irrelevancy of our
times, is that in a few short years after 1450 a conjuncture of factors.

which gave Europe a slight edge over other areas, transformed the world from a motley collection of unrelated feudalisms into a new system we call capitalist world-economy with the *core* and the *periphery* already formed, and distinct from the *external arena*.[36] The core produced very highly valued goods; the periphery was that geographical sector that produced primarily low ranking goods; and the external arena, while awaiting its incorporation into the system at the periphery status, exchanged preciosities for the core's "pacotille."[37] In its present form, the system is divided into the centre and the periphery.

The main premise of the world-system methodology is, therefore, exactly what Wallerstein says it is, when he describes it as:

> The arena within which social action takes place and social change occurs is not 'society' in the abstract, but a definite 'world', a spatio-temporal whole, whose spatial scope is co-extensive with the elementary division of labour among its constituent regions or parts ... specifically, this arena ... has been and continues to be the modern world-system, which emerges in the sixteenth century as a European-centred world-economy.[38]

While this modern world-system emerged in the sixteenth century as a European-centred world-economy, the history of this world-system is more than the history of Europe. It is larger than European history, in that while European history may have been initiating and is dominant, the history of the modern world-system attempts to marry the different and conflicting interests, fates, and involvements of both Europeans and non-Europeans in their "world-wide" and unitary contexts. It attempts to study this history along the singular axis of the development of the modern world-economy, as it is uniquely described by the emergence of the conscious and methodological pursuit of accumulating capital in the centre and away from the periphery.

The methodology in question conceives the world-system as capitalist simply because the world-wide economic form upon which it is based is considered capitalist. The methodology attributes a definite historicity to the capitalist world-system. It tends to take an evolutionary perspective of the development of the world-system in both its intensive and extensive aspects. In particular, this methodology considers the dominant historic theme — the historical theme of themes which gives the system its historic identity — to be the accumulation of capital on an ever-increasing secular scale, cyclical variations notwithstanding. The area covered by the ever-increasing scale of capital accumulation is regarded to be coterminous with the increasing worldization and the intensification of the nascent European capitalism which began in the late fifteenth century as a result of the crisis of European feudalism at that time. This methodology places great emphasis on the process of unequal incidence of accumulating capital on a world scale as between the centre and the periphery of the world-economy. The world-system methodology makes the singular claim that it is not possible to discuss any aspects of the human and the societal realities without taking into account the historic identity of the capitalist world-system. The identity of this system is to be understood in the general terms of its nature, characteristic structures and processes, its marked tendencies, contradictions, antinomies, and paradoxes.[39]

Oliver Cox put it very well, when he stated:

To the social scientist, nothing could be more important than an understanding of the nature of capitalism. All major contemporary social change involves, essentially, processes of the capitalist system — a system so pervasive that, by the opening of the twentieth century, the life of practically every individual on earth had been brought within its purview. Mankind has known no comparable culture; and, most remarkable, it probably cannot be shown that the system originated and became viable as a "natural" consequence of historical evolution.[40]

European feudalism may or may not have produced it, but that hardly matters. As Cox continues, "... capitalism, as a system of societies, is characterized by a definable order and structure which not only differentiates it from other social systems, but also determines and limits interactions of persons within its reach."[41]

The methodology shares the view that the capitalist world-system will not endure forever, because, like all other social systems, it cannot be programmed to do so. Few will disagree with the position that world capitalism will give way to some other social form, because, as the capitalist system develops, its structural fatigue also develops and, as a result, its inner contradictions become increasingly irreconcilable and a breaking point is bound to be reached. Precisely, *when* and *how* the system will collapse and exactly *what* will replace it are the most interesting questions in political economy, even dominated as it is by bland Eurocentric ideas.

One view is that, as the contradictions in the system intensify, the paradoxes between the capitalist realities and the capitalist myths will become so glaring that the system, as we have come to know it, will be deemed inhuman and unworkable and, therefore, irrational. Human beings will lose faith in it and steer the system's redeemables towards supporting a more viable social form that will already be developing in the old capitalist form.

Another view, advanced by Immanuel Wallerstein and derived from the world-system methodology, is this:

> What provides the continuity of a capitalist world-economy through its *longue durée* is the continuous functioning of its three central antinomies: economy/polity; supply/demand; capital/labour. The coexistence of these three antinomies is defining of capitalism, and the way their contradictions fit into each other is the clue to the dynamics of the system as a whole.[42]

If the three antinomies explain the continuity and the dynamics of the capitalist world-economy in cyclical terms as they are resolved by the system's secular tendencies, then its discontinuity and its eventual transformation can be approached through observing the extent to which their contradictions begin to find it impossible to "fit into each other." The logic behind this reasoning is that the above antinomies relate to four secular tendencies, namely the process of *expansion*, the process of *proletarianization*, the process of *politicization*, and the process of the *janissarization* of the ruling class. These tendencies have asymptotic properties,[43] and as the limits approach, the objective bases of transition would become clear. Meanwhile, as the system evolves and as we understand it much better, we should be able to increasingly distinguish, with some sophistication and sensitivity, mere *anti-régime* forces from real *anti-systemic* forces.[44] The world-system methodology appears to have the capacity to aid the appreciation of this vital distinction.

To appreciate the world-system methodology and its overall implications, it is very important to realize that the world-economy is called capitalist, not because all the different economic forms which compose it are *equally*, in the sense of *identically*, capitalist, but because the dominance in the world-economy is capitalist. This means that the imperatives of the world-economy obey the dictates of the historic theme of world-wide accumulation of capital in the centre and away from the periphery, without prejudice to the enforced participation in this economy by other modes of production in their subordinate and exploited roles.

Samir Amin expresses the matter well, when he says:

The concept of "mode of production" is an abstract one, implying no historical order of sequence with respect to the entire period of the history of civilizations that stretches from the first differentiated formations right down to capitalism.[45]

He adds that no mode of production has ever existed in a pure state:

The societies known to history are "formations" that on the one hand combine modes of production and on the other organize relations between the local societies and other societies, expressed in the existence of long-distance trade relations.

Social formations are thus concrete organized structures that are marked by a dominant mode of production and the articulation around this is of a complex group of modes of production that are subordinate to it.[46]

Central to the world-system methodology is the importance accorded the role of markets in the development and operation of the capitalist world-economy. In this connection, the argument should not be allowed to degenerate into a vulgar contest for primacy between the importance of markets on the one hand and the articulation between the levels of the development forces of production and production relations on the other, in the development of world capitalism. The argument is simply that it is not possible to consider the development of the capitalist world-economy without considering the essential part played in this development by "world" trade from the very beginning. It is excessively Eurocentric to argue that European capitalism could have developed without world markets and world trade. The capitalist world-economy, which Europe initiated, did not develop without world markets. To argue that markets were not important in the development of capitalism is to relegate to the realm of the unimportant the essential roles played in the development of capitalism by the non-European parts of the world. From this, it is but a short step to the absurd argument that in our contemporary present some capitalisms do not need trade!

The question should never be whether surplus value can be realized with or without external non-capitalist markets. The concerns which this question betrays are the Eurocentric preoccupations with the purity of the European capitalist mode of production. In the world-system methodology, the concern is not with the purity of any mode of production, but with *the nature of the very impurity of the capitalist formation at the world level*: the articulation of different modes of production as it has served the course of world capitalist formation from its earliest times in the late fifteenth century till now.

Expanded reproduction may or may not be possible without external markets, but that is not the question. The "product" may or may not be realizable, with or without external markets, which question may even be "nonsense," according to Lenin,[47] but that is not the point. It may or may not be *"inherent* in capitalist production to strive for unlimited expansion"[48] but that does not matter. It becomes the question and it matters in history only from the Eurocentric point of view, where the historiographic mistake has always been to confuse the dominance of the European mode of production with the world capitalist formation itself. From the world-system perspective, there is no question about it: real world-history shows that the world capitalist formation did not develop without the involvements of the non-European parts of the world through the search for and the development of markets of all kinds. This is the simple fact that world-system sources have attempted to make clear.[49] The message from the world-system perspective, indeed the basis of the world-system methodology, is that the world-system, and the world-economy which supports it, cannot adequately be studied if they are perceived as capitalistically pure and isolated in the setting of a closed system.[50] To emphasize this point, I shall make the deceptively absurd statement that the only closed system since the late fifteenth century has been the capitalist world-system in evolution.

I should make it clear that the world-system methodology, as in all other methodologies, does not only owe a lot to other methodological sources, it is also based on thin strands of reasoning. Essentially, the world-system methodology, while it is free, like other methodologies, to claim a lot for itself, is based on no more than the thin strand of reasoning which conceives of the modern world as a definite system, a definite historical system, with an undisputed identity of its own. It conceives of the world as larger than, and it implies the conception of the modern world as, a system of societal units, however defined. It relates these units and significant groups within them one to the other in ways which indicate how and why this *real* system affects and shapes all else in it, from the environment through the individual to the nation-state. Herein lies the methodological novelty and usefulness of the world-system approach to the reality problem, as I pose it above in terms of the continuity of imperialism.

Given this, I suggest that, among other things, the world-system perspective would insist upon the following: first, that concepts which appear to be specific to the "world" must be approached in terms of their relevance to the understanding of the vitalities and the dynamics of the modern world-system, the capitalist world-system; second, that such concepts should be seen in terms of their contrasting world-system origins and precedents; and third, that the world-system must be approached first and foremost in terms of its essential economic foundation realities, its political and other social aspects, as important as they are in their own right, notwithstanding.[51]

From the above, we suggest that the concept imperialism is the most vibrant, and for this reason the most adequate, concept for relating the diverse experiences of the different "world" in their spatio-temporal senses and within the world-economy into the coherent time- and history-specific whole which the world-system perspective postulates. It is only within the world-system frame that the full analytic richness of the concept imperialism can be appreciated. Within this frame, the concept imperialism cannot, and it does not, pretend to stand on its own. It comes into its analytic own when it is called upon to relate the changes in the specific history of the modern world-system to the changes in its economy. And this is how it does it: within the world-system frame, the concept imperialism accounts for the historically specific origins and development of augmented inequality and induced over-dependence, both of which mutually buttress exploitation of some by others for the one supreme purpose characteristic of, and unique to, the modern world-system, the accumulation, but unequal incidence, of capital through the medium of production, not so much for immediate use as for sale on a world market, the characteristics of production and final consumption being achieved along certain lines of "elementary division of labour among (the world's) constituent regions and parts."[52]

Seen in the world-system context, the arguments which cling to the much-repeated liberal call for the suppression of the concept imperialism in scientific endeavours, because of its presumed unscientific nature, and the radical and Marxist views of the concept, which give rise to this call, can be clearly seen for what they are: Eurocentric arguments about Eurocentric renditions of a world-system concept.

Let me explain. As I understand it, the world-system perspective does not attempt to belittle European dominance in the unfolding of world-history. It recognizes, and it concedes to, European dominance. What it does not do, however, is to slight other histories within world-history by virtue of the recognition of, and the concession to, European dominance. The world-system's distinctiveness, indeed its epistemological point of departure, lies in the attention it draws to non-European histories by focusing on the dynamic interface between these histories and the dominating European history.

The world-system perspective, in fact its methodology, is the study of the evolution of the process of unequal *interdependence-interaction* between the parts of an "enlarging" and certainly an intensifying world. If initially what triggered off our modern world-system were internal European crises of decadent feudalism, what constitute the modern world are the following: the *changes* that the initial European expansion brought about in the different feudalisms in other parts of the world, the changes which occurred in Europe as a result of these initial contacts, and how these many *changes* have come to assume a character of their own, which is so all-embracing and so all-affective that few events in any part of the world today, if any, can be appreciated fully without reference to the ever-changing nature of the relations brought about by the initial European expansion.

From the point of view of what I have called the reality problem, the structural-relationals which constitute the emergent world are ever-changing and yet, paradoxically, they appear to remain essentially the same. They are ever-changing because the "European spaces" in the world have been expanding while the "non-European spaces" in it have been shrinking. The forms and the mechanisms of these complex sets of relations, which make up the world, have themselves been changing. However, in effect, they remain essentially the same, in the sense that the realization of the historic theme of the modern world has always favoured Europe.

My understanding of the world-system indicates to me that if the common concept of imperialism is a historic(al) concept, which it is, it is maximally utilized as such only when it is made to account for the paradox of the ever-changing forms and mechanisms of the relations and the interrelations which constitute the world-economy, and how they explain the constancy of its historic theme — the unequal incidence of accumulating capital.

The basic postulate of the world-system methodology is really very simple. It is that the world is a system, that the history of this system is definite and clear, and that, in the pursuit of its historic theme, its logic embraces the logics of all its subparts.

Approaching the Thesis

It is this composite historic logic that the concept of imperialism amply describes, in that the concept is capable of framing the precise processual context within which to understand the relational peculiarities which define the secular stages of the world-system with respect to its capitalist *development* and its dialectical counterpart of capitalist *underdevelopment*.

The argument is that, if the virtue of the concept of imperialism, for this purpose, lies in its potential ability to relate the developmental consequences of the historical process of capital accumulation, then with respect to underdevelopment, its virtue lies precisely in its potential ability to relate the inner processes of the exploitative consequent of world capitalism. These inner processes are those *augmenting unequal* incidence of accumulated capital and those *inducing dependency* by depriving periphery societies of the internal ability to accumulate capital. These two sets of processes underpin capitalism, the exploitation process which expresses itself, in the final analysis, as the unequal incidence of accumulating capital as between the centre and the periphery.[53]

Put another way, it is to say that, from the third world perspective, the concept imperialism is most apt for framing the precise processual context within which to understand the persistence of the relational peculiarities and particularities which define the secular stages of the world-system with respect to the development-underdevelopment dialectic. The virtue of the concept, for this purpose, lies in its potential ability to situate and at the same time relate the real consequences of the historical process of capitalist development within its own world-wide and expansionist history. It is to say that these consequences are summed up by the properties of *augmenting inequality* and *induced dependency*. These two factors operate mutually to buttress capitalist exploitation for the singular purpose of facilitating capital accumulation in the centre and away from the periphery of the world-system.

However, the use to which the concept imperialism has been put so far necessitates some fundamental revisions towards a new synthesis, within the modern world-system perspective, if it is to perform the functions of framing world-history, and at the same time serve as the key term around which to examine and assess the reality of the costs to the non-European areas of the world, arising as a result of their involvement in the world-history of capital accumulation. All this, it must be said, is to provoke discussion on *real* development: transitional alternatives within the transformation of the present world order.

Generally, scholars write on the subject of imperialism mainly because they want to prosecute or defend history. Such prosecution or defence of history, however, serves very little purpose. This is because, while it is true that history has committed some atrocious crimes in its course, the transformational belief is still extant that history, as a process, can be rehabilitated enough to make its past deeds — history as fact — pardonable. It is in this regard that Obi Egbuna put it very well when he said, "... the knowledge of one's mistakes is the secret of survival."[54] And we may well add that for all social systems, including the world-system, the "secret of survival" means nothing if not the creative and continual rehabilitation of the social system's history. But then, rehabilitation is possible only after a proper knowledge of the undesirable aspects of a system's history. This much we must admit without hesitation or contention.

My present concern is to move towards a review[55] of world-history in such a way that the crimes for which this history, in its relevant duration, must definitely be indicted will be seen in their proper relief. I intend to attempt a new synthesis of the historical concept of imperialism, my purpose being to pave the way for the incorporation into the idea associated in the newly synthesized conception of imperialism of those ideas normally associated with the concepts *development* and *underdevelopment*. The very ideas associated with these two concepts appear to be going through crises of relevance and confidence;[56] and here the suspicion for this is that the concepts are largely treated ahistorically and Eurocentrically. The suggestion here is that by approaching development through a historically reviewed and newly-synthesized conception of imperialism, we can approach the concept of development from its proper *ontological* referents; and, therefore, be in a position to take a glimpse at its *axiology*. This will make it possible for us, at the theoretical level at least, to attempt the correct resolution of the crisis in which the idea of development finds itself.

In pursuit of this aim, I take particular exception to three blatant inaccuracies in modern thought, that: (1) imperialism, as a reality of historical relevance, dates only from the late nineteenth century; (2) it is as old as the history of man; and (3) the concept must be dismembered into its economic, political, cultural, strategic, and other components to be understood analytically and hence to be historically useful.

I object, in particular, to the first inaccuracy, according to which imperialism is thought to be only a product of "mature," or the industrial phase of, capitalism. By this view, imperialism is not considered to be related in any interesting way to the earlier phases of capitalism.

My contention here argues against these views of imperialism as being unsupported by facts, as they occurred in their peculiarly distinct forms in modern history. I propose that such understandings of imperialism can be maintained only by obsessive preoccupation with the interests of the core countries of the world. In support of the above and as already indicated, I cast my argument in terms of a critical interpretation of the intensifying awareness of capitalism as an evolutionary process at the world level to advance the following thesis: *insofar as imperialism is in any way related to the externalization of European capitalism, leading to its globalization of the world-system, imperialism has been around in various forms, and has metamorphosized with the capitalist world-economy, ever since its initial emergence in Europe in the late fifteenth century.*

This is what I have called the *continuity of capitalist imperialism thesis.*

The character of the present world-system owes more to the emergence and the development of capitalism than to any other demonstrable cause. The fact that today we have a single world-system with unavoidable and unequal interdependence among its multi-level and various groups, that we have a dangerously advanced technology, and that the demographic pattern of the world has changed so drastically since the late fifteenth century, are all due to the development of the capitalist world-economy. My initial position within the world-system methodology is that these novel historical "departures" began to take form at the same time that the nascent capitalist forces in Europe began to push for the world-wide exploration which led to the many "discoveries" and to the varying modes of domination and exploitation over the entire course of modern history.

Seen from the world-society, rather than from the European-society, perspective, imperialism seems to be "an abiding attribute of capitalism."[57] This makes the nature of imperialism crystal clear. It also paves the way for a new and more historically precise synthesis of the concept. This would make it possible for the concept to be formalized in a way which could serve as the basis for a first approximate detection of changes in the very structural-relational deformities which define the world-system, as such, as underdeveloped.

In all respects, most of the existing arguments on imperialism are long-winded and distractive of the relevant historical continuity. By and large, the arguments have been presented in such ways as to suggest that either the ideas associated with the concept are intrinsically complex and confusing, or, as one can very easily come to suspect, that these ideas are deliberately made to appear so for Eurocentric purposes.

From the world-system perspective, the debates on the concept seem to have been conducted in the most curious terms of poor historical periodization. I believe that those who consider the phenomenon to be as old as the history of *homo sapiens* are not being as sensitive as they should be to the historic consistency within the identity of the world capitalist historicity. They are *imprecise* in their definition of imperialism. They ignore completely the uniqueness of the capitalist origins of the profound transformation of the history of the world from the many *unrelated "localized" histories to a world-history of every-growing interrelatedness.*[58] And I believe further that those who see imperialism as a phenomenon connected historically only with the industrial phase of European capitalism are being much too cavalier with the defining consistency of the history of world capitalism. They are over-sensitive to the limited identities of the different "contexts of conjuncture" in this very history; and they are too insensitive to the historic consistency of this history. This is what makes this conception of imperialism *over-precise*. Seen as a phenomenon of relevance only since the late nineteenth century, this view of imperialism does not cover the earlier crucial periods of the pre-1870s during which the capitalist form of economy took shape and became what was generally considered "mature" by the 1870s. The crucial non-European-world inputs of the earlier periods to capitalist development and the accumulation process are ignored as being no more than *pre-capitalist*.

The period 1500–1870 should not be treated so benignly by the first view and so indistinguishably by the second, for this was the period during which the pressures from the crisis in European feudalism dictated the great explorations which led to the great "discoveries" and the great plunders, which in their turn lead to the termination of "unrelated localized" histories in the world and to the initiation of "interrelated local" histories through the establishment of the Euro-American, the Euro-African, and the Euro-Asian connections on the permanent and problematic bases, as we know them today.[59]

Surely, by the late nineteenth century, capitalism had done much more to the different parts of the world than merely served them notice of its presence and of its intention to replace or affect other feudalisms in the world.

It is true that capitalism had done many profound things to Europe during the few hundred years of its development prior to the late nineteenth century. But it is even more true that capitalism had, through Europe, done more profound things to the rest of the world. By the late nineteenth century, the world had long ceased to look like what it was before the end of the fifteenth century. By this date, the indigenous peoples of the Americas and the Caribbean Islands were all but completely killed off, and the full incorporation of India into the capitalist world-system was well under way; by this date, the accessible parts of the African coasts, having served the slave trade so well, were providing the footholds and the bridgeheads needed for further European expansion inland; and the southern part of Africa was already occupied by people of European stock. By this date, too, frantic efforts and stratagems were under way to ensure China's inclusion in what had long ceased to be a European economy. What the world had in the 1870s, whatever else it did not have aside, was a *world-economy*, an economy centred in Europe but which needed distant parts of the world to thrive.[60]

This economic form is called capitalist because it produced not so much for "local" markets and for immediate consumption, but for "world-wide" markets; it produced as a basis for further production; it completely separated the producer from the means of production in some parts of the world and it incorporated other modes of production relations in other parts of the world. The dynamics of the economic system were motivated by the need for profits for the supreme purpose of accumulating capital to serve further production. Whatever else may be disputed in this regard, what is not to be disputed is that this capitalist world-economy did not just happen to be what it was, mature or industrial, in 1870. It had a history which had already changed the world by the late nineteenth century and which promised, by its expansionary real history,[61] to change it even more.

However, with imperialism, it is not possible to separate one question from another. The answer to the question of what imperialism is always implies the answer to the question of what causes it, and *vice-versa*. In a broad sense, there are three discernible traits to the many treatments given these two related questions, namely the Marxist, the radical, and the liberal treatments. In the *Marxist* camp, we include all who claim the works of Marx and Engels — classical Marxism — as their source of inspiration and ideas. The *radicals* are those whose arguments indicate, in their vitalities, that they have read Marx and Engels but have ended by formulating their positions fundamentally against some of the pet Marxist tenets. The *liberals* are those whose writings aim expressly to counter the Marxist position. They aim either to demolish the Marxist arguments and/or to substitute for them. In our terms, the methodological and the motivational commonality between all these treatments is what we have described as Eurocentric.

It is the Eurocentric contentions between these three schools of thought which have given the concept imperialism that layer upon layer of complexity which appeals variously to history, logic, and ideologies, and which, as a result, has endowed the concept with that surrealistic blend of Eurocentric fluidity and rigidity: *imprecision* and *over-precision*.

However, the debate on imperialism, no matter how bizarre it may appear, centres, in the main, on three issues. They are: whether imperialism is caused essentially by economic rather than political or socio-psychological factors and considerations; if so, whether these factors are associated in any way with a particular economic form and its inner laws, to wit, whether capitalism is to blame for imperialism in the modern sense, or whether imperialism is only spuriously related to capitalism by fallacious reasoning bred by conspiracy of ideology. Implied in this, is the question of whether imperialism of modern times differs from that of older times. From the two points above emerges the third point at issue, which is whether imperialism, as a matter of both history and theory, is a policy option *chosen* by "groups" or an *inescapable and inherent* part of group action, once certain, or more precisely, particular historical or theoretical logicalities are reached. Co-ordinated answers to these questions tell us what one thinks about imperialism, but the clinging question, sheared of its didactic meanderings, is: *whether the so-called modern imperialism (post-1870s), to the extent that it differs from the so-called old imperialism, is a policy or an inescapable consequence of capitalism, and, if the latter, what inner logic of capitalism impels this imperialist inevitability?*

This summary question, as useful as it might have been for the restricted study of historical materialism from the Eurocentric perspective, we contend, is the wrong question. The real question, we propose, should be: *so as to understand our contemporary world situation historically, and therefore much better for the purpose of transforming it, whether (capitalist) imperialism — capitalist expansion, domination, and exploitation on a world scale in pursuit of capital accumulation in the centre and away from the periphery — should not be distinguished from any other previous phenomenon of falsely kindred character; and whether capitalist imperialism should not, therefore, date from the fifteenth century.*

Put this way, it is the uniqueness of the capitalist origins and its development through its history, world-history, and its unique implications for the world as a whole that are made the subjects of enquiry. The value of such an enquiry lies in the fact that it can tell us *how* and *why* our contemporary world came to be what it is; and it can help explain the tendential properties of the world-system, using the world as a unit and focusing on its historical developmental process, rather than seeing the world, as such, as merely an unimportant arena for the secondary expressions of a part of it, even if this part is the dominant part. Viewed this way, attention is drawn to the capitalist globalization of the world as both a historical process and a historical fact. It, then, becomes possible to disengage from the (by no means uninteresting) debate as to whether imperialism is a policy or an inescapable consequence of capitalism; and it becomes possible to concentrate on imperialism as a fact of capitalist world-history. The key question, as raised above, makes it possible to concentrate analytic attention on the constancies and on the variations in the capitalist ethos at the world level, the changing forms and the constant effect of imperialism, and on the varying intensities of the forces which propel it along and toward the goals of exploitation and polarization on a world scale.

The pity of the situation is that despite the ferocity of the debate on imperialism, the above question is not addressed very often. Any work, therefore, which intends to use the evolution of world-history, as it is embodied in the world-expansion implications of capitalism, as a point of departure for the study of the contemporary state and tendencies of world development, will find very little outside the few world-system sources to go by in the vast and varied literature on the subject of imperialism.

It is true that familiarity with the subject cautions for its vastness, but it also saddens for its glaring irrelevance to the key question as formulated above. But then, for these very same reasons, familiarity with the subject could encourage one towards the clarification of the concept's essence, through the realization that neither the fluidity nor the rigidity of a concept's usage at any given time is necessarily a pointer to that concept's usefulness as an analytic tool.

A historical concept is a concept the usage of which is intrinsically bound up with social history and the variations within it. Historical concepts, to have any meaning at all, must be used in historically precise contexts. They must be used in the context of their strict historicities which contain their relevant historicals. The aim in the analysis of a historical concept, then, must be to lay bare the historical "real meaning" of the concept. In this exercise what is needed is the ability to distinguish between something appearing to be changing and yet remaining the same, and something appearing to remain the same yet changing. Knowing this is the secret to the dialectical understanding of social history.

Imperialism is a historical concept. And believing, as I do here, that the analysis of any historical concept is bound to be trite if the analysis is based solely on the changing or constant superficialities of the concept's ontology, it is in order to call attention to the fact that, if the analysis of a historical concept means anything at all, the analysis is obliged to make maximum allowances for the historical variations in the concept's essential attributes within its specific historicity. Historical sensitivity is all that the analysis of a historical concept is about and, therefore, what makes historical analysis worth pursuing is the eloquence with which the congruence of variations within the attributes of the concept do, or do not, speak to the continuity of history seen through appearances in history's changing contexts of conjunction.

Notes

1. Paul A. Baran, *The Political Economy of Growth* (Modern Reader Paperbacks, New York, 1968), p. 137, states, with respect to the conditions from which

capitalism evolved in both the present advanced and the present underdeveloped parts of the world: "These were everywhere a mode of production and a social and political order that are conveniently summarized under the name feudalism. Not that the structure of feudalism was everywhere the same. Quite on the contrary, just as 'one would be right in talking, not of a single history of capitalism, and of the general shape which this has, but of a collection of histories of capitalism, all of them having a general similarity of shape, but each of them separately dated as regards its main stages' [Maurice Dobb, *Studies in the Development of Capitalism* (London, 1946), p. 21], so one has to bear in mind the tremendous difference between the histories of the feudal systems in different parts of the world."

Samir Amin takes these differences further in his *Unequal Development: An Essay on the Social Formation of Peripheral Capitalism* (Harvester Press, Sussex, 1976), and his *Class and Nation, Historically and in the Current Crisis* (Monthly Review Press, New York, 1980), where he distinguishes between "weak" and "strong" feudalisms and explains the emergence of capitalism in Europe through the "feudal crisis" in terms of the comparative "weakness" of European feudalism; and where he distinguishes between central, state, and peripheral types of capitalism constituting the world capitalist formation.

2. For an example of what seems to be this type of history, see Giovanni Arrighi, *The Geometry of Imperialism: The Limits of Hobson's Paradigm* (NLB, London, 1978).

3. Discussing Hobson's theory of imperialism, Arrighi (see note 2 above, pp. 50–51), says that "if the concept of imperialism is identified ... with the image of hegemony, there undoubtedly appears to be a fundamental continuity in English foreign policy — not only, as Gallagher and Robinson argue, through the nineteenth century, but, as we shall see shortly, during the two hundred and fifty years between the mid-seventeenth century and the beginning of the nineteenth century." He then goes on to add, "In conceding this, we need not renounce the attempt to identify, within the drive for hegemony pursued by a given power, either the *overall* direction of alterations or accentuations of its components in different periods, or above all, the diverse meanings which the same policy may acquire according to the concrete situation."
   Also, Lenin, in his *Imperialism: The Highest Stage of Capitalism* (International Publishers, New York, 1969), suggests in passing that the concept could apply to the 300 years preceding the 1900s.
   None of these two views push the historicity of the concept back far enough for our world-system purposes.

4. J. Gallagher and R. Robinson, "Imperialism of Free Trade," *Economic History Review*, Series 2, vol. 6, no. 1 (1953).

5. Roger Owen and Bob Sutcliffe, eds., *Studies in the Theory of Imperialism* (Longman, London, 1972). All the essays in this volume are open to this charge, with the partial exception of Ronald Robinson's "Non-European Foundations of European Imperialism: Sketch for a Theory of Collaboration," pp. 117–142, and the clear exception of Thomas Hodgkin's "Some African and Third World Theories of Imperialism," pp. 93–116.

6. I return to this matter in chapter five.

7. This particular insight is crucial for seeing each specific expression of imperialism as a two-way graduating process, an indication that imperialism involved sections of the imperialized people. It is also a pointer to the important fact that once imperialism was introduced in any particular instance it did not become only part of a local history, it also linked or related a local history to other local histories within the evolving world-history of related localized histories. See Terence Hopkins' reference to the formation of Uganda in his "World-System Analysis: Methodological Issues," in Barbara Hockey Kaplan,

ed., *Social Change in the Capitalist World Economy* (Sage Publications, London, 1978), pp. 216–217.

8. In Owen and Sutcliffe (see note 5 above), pp. 93–116.

9. Hodgkin (see note 5 above), p. 93. That such theories are by Europeans may have a lot to do with their being Eurocentric, but some Eurocentric theories of imperialism are by non-Europeans. See, for example, Kwame Nkrumah, *Neo-Colonialism: The Last Stage of Imperialism* (Heinemann, Ibadan, 1968). Nkrumah subscribes to the Hobson-Lenin view on the periodization of imperialism within the capitalist historicity as a late nineteenth century phenomenon (see pp. 31, 43, 77, 79, and passim).

10. Hodgkin (see note 5 above), p. 95.

11. Hodgkin (see note 5 above), p. 95.

12. Hodgkin (see note 5 above), p. 98.

13. Exploitation is one of the most commonly abused concepts in the Eurocentric tradition. From this perspective, either exploitation does not exist at all within the capitalist historicity, or it has always been with man in history, or it applies only to the extraction of surplus value produced by those who have been separated from their means of production and are therefore forced to sell their labour power. The only Eurocentric justification for the last sense of exploitation is that it is considered a *category*. And as a category, this is what Eurocentrics say it should mean, implying that earlier forms of dispossession and unequal distribution in the earlier phases of world capital formation cannot strictly be considered exploitation — plunder and "legal theft," perhaps, but not exploitation. That this category, among many, is wholly external to the real history of capital formation that it claims to illuminate is ignored by Eurocentrics.

14. Hodgkin (see note 5 above), pp. 99–100.

15. Samir Amin, *Accumulation on a World Scale: A Critique of the Theory of Underdevelopment*, vol. 2 (Monthly Review Press, New York, 1974), p. 597.

16. Samir Amin, *Imperialism and Unequal Development* (Monthly Review Press, New York, 1977), p. 103.

17. Amin (see note 15 above), p. 22; also note 1 above, pp. 75 and 168.

18. Samir Amin, "The Early Roots of Unequal Exchange," *Monthly Review* 27, no. 7 (1975): 43–47.

19. The reader is referred to the numerous works by Andre Gunder Frank on the subject, especially his *World Accumulation, 1492–1789* and his *Dependent Accumulation and Underdevelopment* (Macmillan, London, 1978), and his recent book on *Crisis*, vols. 1 and 2 (Holmes and Meier, London, 1980).

20. Frank (see note 19 above), pp. 238–239.

21. See his essays in his *Latin America: Underdevelopment or Revolution* (Monthly Review Press, New York, 1969).

22. Frank (see note 19 above), pp. 238–271.

23. See his essay, "From Feudalism to Capitalism: Transition or Transitions," and "The Rise and Future Demise of the World Capitalist System: Concepts for Comparative Analysis," in his *The Capitalist World-Economy* (Cambridge University Press, London 1979), pp. 1–36.

24. Johan Galtung, *Methodology and Ideology: Theory and Method of Social Research* (Christian Ejlers, Copenhagen, 1977), p. 14.

25. Frank (see note 19 above), p. 13. In an earlier draft of this book, Frank expressed this idea even better: theory = history.

26. Immanuel Wallerstein, *The Modern World-System: Capitalist Agriculture and the Origins of European World Economy in the Sixteenth Century* (Academic Press, New York, 1976), p. xi.

27. Wallerstein (see note 26 above), pp. xi–xii.

28. Wallerstein (see note 26 above), p. 9.

29. Wallerstein (see note 26 above), p. 27.
30. Wallerstein (see note 26 above), p. 15.
31. Wallerstein (see note 26 above), p. 15.
32. Wallerstein (see note 26 above), p. 15.
33. E.J. Hobsbawm, *The Age of Capital, 1848–1875* (Weidenfeld and Nicolson, London, 1975), p. 1.
34. Here I am referring to the cyclical rhythm of its development and the compounding weakening it must have for its eventual demise. See "Special Issue on Cycles and Trends," *Review* 2, no. 4 (1979).
35. Here I mean in the *transformational* final analysis.
36. See Wallerstein (note 26 above) for a fuller discussion.
37. Wallerstein (see note 26 above), pp. 199–200.
38. Terence Hopkins and Immanuel Wallerstein (and Braudel Centre), "Patterns of Development of the Modern World-System, Research Proposal," *Review* 1, no. 2 (1977): 112.
39. For a fuller treatment of this matter, see my "A World-System Critique of Eurocentric Conceptions of Capitalism" (Mimeo, 1980), especially the section on "World-System Methodology: An Interpretation of the Capitalist Identity."
40. Oliver C. Cox, *Capitalism as a System* (Monthly Review Press, New York, 1964), p. ix.
41. Cox (see note 40 above), p. ix.
42. Wallerstein, "A Historical Perspective on the Emergence of the New International Order: Economic, Political, Cultural Aspects," in his *The Capitalist World-Economy* (see note 23 above), p. 272.
43. Wallerstein (see note 42 above), p. 278.
44. I return to this distinction again because it is particularly important that, as part of the transitional realization, we know which forces *really* transform the system and which only mask the decay.
45. Amin (see note 1 above), p. 13.
46. Amin (see note 1 above), p. 16.
47. V.I. Lenin, "On the So-Called Question of Markets," in *Collected Works*, vol. 2 (Progress Publishers, Moscow, 1960), p. 164.
48. Rosa Luxemburg, *The Accumulation of Capital* (Routledge and Kegan Paul, London, 1963).
49. This is a vital point to grasp, if theory is indeed to be history.
50. We are beginning to appreciate what Rosa Luxemburg meant. For a brief statement to this effect, see Amiya Kumar Bagchi, "A Note on the Requirements of a Theory of Imperialism" (Mimeo, 1980).
51. We shall return to this in chapter five.
52. Hopkins and Wallerstein (see note 38 above), p. 112.
53. See my "Toward the Study of International Development: A Proposal," *Caribbean Yearbook of International Relations* (Sijthoff, Leyden, 1976), pp. 465–489.
54. Obi B. Egbune, *Emperor of the Sea* (Fontana, Glasgow, 1975), p. 74.
55. It is important here not to confuse the *reviewing* of history with the *rewriting* of it.
56. For a fuller discussion of this matter, see the UNU/GPID publication, Herb Addo et al., *Development as Social Transformation: Reflections on the Global Problematique* (Hodder and Stoughton, London, 1985).
57. Cox (see note 40 above), p. 136.
58. This distinction is crucial to the appreciation of the identity of the world-system methodology.
59. See Eric Williams, *From Columbus to Castro: The History of the Caribbean 1492–1969* (Andre Deutsch, London, 1978), pp. 13–18.

60. The users of the world-system methodology tend to agree on this point. It is, however, Wallerstein's recent works that have given this fact the increasing prominence it deserves in the literature.
61. At this point, it matters very little whether capitalism expands as of necessity or by choice. We are referring here to the expansionary fact of its real history.

Part Two

World-System Critiques

Chapter Three

The Liberal Conception of Imperialism

The Basic Liberal Argument

In dealing with the Eurocentric charge with respect to the liberal conception of imperialism, we shall point to this conception's intellectual source of origin, raise some pertinent queries, make some observations from our viewpoint, and see how liberals have tended to respond to them. But, to really make our case against the liberals, we shall subject a recent grand statement of the liberal view to some severe criticism, in order to show that to the extent that our queries and observations cannot be responded to adequately by the liberal arguments, to that extent our charge that the liberal conception of imperialism is Eurocentric is valid.

Liberals tend to take after Joseph Schumpeter in the ontology of the concept. In this regard, they reject outright any association of imperialism with economic determinants. Schumpeter defines imperialism as an "objectless disposition on the part of a state to unlimited forcible expansion."[1] From this view, liberals naturally come to consider it a basic fallacy to view imperialism as a necessary phase of capitalism, or even to suggest that capitalism could develop into imperialism, the reason being that imperialism's very *objectless* purpose goes against the very grain of capitalist rationality, by which entrepreneurs, the carriers of the capitalist spirit, have less reason to engage in "objectless expansion" than to make profit under peaceful and stable conditions.[2]

In addition to the term *unlimited*, the other key terms in this conception of imperialism are: *objectless*, *state*, and *forcible*, all particularizing *expansion*. The first problem is how to interpret the term unlimited. How *unlimited* is "unlimited" expansion? Or did Schumpeter mean "unending" or "unceasing"[3] expansion rather than "unlimited"? Perhaps *unlimited* is to be understood in close relation to *objectless*. This is the only way in which the term unlimited can make sense in the definitional context, since, surely, at any one time there is a limit to any state's expansion, in both senses of *extensive* and *intensive* expansion. In which case, by unlimited, he meant, perhaps, in *pretensions.*

The use of the term *state* itself poses a problem. The state, as we have come to know of its development, has not always been around in its modern form. This raises the problem of how we precisely date the kind of state expansion in Schumpeter's definition. If we take the state in the modern sense, the conception becomes suspect, for then it mysteriously becomes that only the modern state indulges in objectless expansion; and if we take the state in the trans-epochal sense, then imperialism becomes timeless. In the first case, imperialism becomes capitalist, since the state, in its modern form, is an integral part of capitalist development; and in the second case, one imperialism becomes indistinguishable from another, and therefore, the concept becomes historico-analytically *imprecise.*

There is also the problem of Schumpeter's use of *forcible.* Obviously, by this term, he meant war. But since there are many kinds of force, some of which can be as effective, if not as efficient, as war can be for the purpose of state expansion, we are left with the strange possibility of not regarding as imperialist any state expansion initiated, or maintained, by means other than war.

Schumpeter's notion of imperialism means, then, that a state involved in an expansion, which can be considered limited and which has an objective — any objective — but which is realized by means other than war, cannot be considered imperialist. This is clearly untenable.

There are some abiding puzzles inherent in Schumpeter's conception. It is not just why *objectless* expansions occur in history, since nothing less than viewing imperialism as a sort of permanent madness in history can resolve this aspect of the puzzle. The bigger puzzle is: Why should imperialism, as seen in Schumpeterian terms, occur in the capitalist age, where it is claimed to be irrational because it is against the capitalist rationality? Schumpeter answers this question with the escapist simplicity that the "dead always rule the living."[4] However, before one can compose oneself enough to ask whether the living ever rule themselves, that is, whether there are instances in which the living ever ignore the irrationalities of the past and justify their actions in terms of their own circumstances, Schumpeter seeks refuge in social and individual psychology. He says, "Imperialism falls into that large group of surviving features ... that play such an important part in every concrete social situation."[5] He continues, "... put in terms of the economic interpretation of history ... it is an atavism in the social structure, in individual psychological habits of emotional reaction."[6]

This is the foundation of the liberal view of imperialism. This is the basis from which other liberals have attempted to add to, or revise, Schumpeter's statement of the liberal line on imperialism. Such names as Winslow, Arendt, Koebner, Landes, Strachey, Fieldhouse, and Cohen, to name but a few, readily come to mind.[7] All these writers seem to agree that whatever else imperialism may or may not be, it is a sort of a mysterious political phenomenon which expresses itself in aggression and war. Winslow, for example, after a brilliant review (by all standards) of what imperialism is said to be by others, concludes on the disappointing note that it is a political phenomenon, an irrational and atavistic *choice* of policy.[8] Arendt simply equates imperialism with totalitarianism. Koebner insists that until certain unprovables are proven, imperialism is best considered a phenomenon as old as the history of man. And Landes, hinging his view of imperialism on the analysis-evading "equilibrium analysis," comes to the amazing conclusion that imperialism exists because "power, like nature, abhors a vacuum."[9] Cohen, in a 1974 publication, sees the whole question of imperialism as being only the product of "the good old game of power politics." He advances the unoriginal and evasive view that the logic of domination derives directly from the existence of competing national sovereignties.[10] In Strachey's case, he sees the granting of independence to the colonial territories in the post-Second World War era as "the end of Imperialism."[11]

As surprising as it may seem, this is the naïve way liberal thinkers handle the subject of imperialism. Their contributions are offered at so high a level of abstraction that they take us nowhere near meaningful comment on the subject. Magdoff is right, therefore, when he says that they contribute nothing to an understanding of historical differences in types and purposes of aggression and expansion.[12] In short, they are insensitive to the subtleties of "historical contexts of conjecture." It is this insensitivity which forms the basis of the charge of Eurocentricity. It is caused by many things, prominent among them being the self-righteous repugnance with which liberals pretend to approach modern wars; and the haste with which they tend to explain them away; and, failing that, their predilection to account for wars as a type of irrational atavism.[13] Let us examine the liberal insensitivity in some detail. But, before we can do this properly, we shall have to agree on some basic points.

It cannot be denied that "states" have expanded in the past in pursuit of many different *motives*, that for expansions to be *meaningful* (even if irrational to some), states must perceive some *reasons* for the expansion, and further, that for the expansion to be *successful* (i.e., for the motives to be attained), states must dominate others *effectively*, even if differently. From the historical perspective, the following questions are, therefore, in order:

1. What have the different (or the differences in) *motives* been?
2. What have (some of) the meaningful *reasons* for expansion been?
3. What have (some of) the *effective means* of domination been to make expansions successful?

Seen from the historically precise analytic perspective, however, the following should be the questions: Taking into consideration the superficialities and substantialities and the constancies and variations in the context of changing human history, if there have been differences in the expansion motives of states, differences in their reasons for expansion, and differences in the effective means of domination employed, can we say that these different factors characterize distinct historical epochs? If so, do certain historically delineated expansion *motives* coincide with certain historically delineated *reasons* for expansion and *means* of effective domination? And, finally, which of these three variables (motives, reasons, or means) is more *historically* definitive?

The relevance and the significance of the above questions are lost to the liberal enquiry into the imperialist phenomenon. The liberals are not sensitive to such questions, because they never intend to go beyond the following: (1) ascribing the irrational love of war as the motive for state expansion; (2) considering war as the only motive of expansion; and (3) regarding war, groundlessly, as the worst of abhorrents.

Accordingly, the first reaction of liberals is to wish war away, as a brand of atavism which will vanish with *time*. *How times differ* from one another and *why they differ* are not regarded as historical problems which must be historically approached from the point of view of precision. They are content merely to explain imperialism in terms of the existence of war-loving elements in states and to hinge the phenomenon on the unapproached cause for the existence of modern states. The fact that the liberal view of the subject does not even consider the historical reasons for the origin and the development of the modern state, and the fact that it cannot even detect the constancies and the variations in historic themes and motives, reasons and means of wars, as they pertain to state expansion, are not considered limitations to the proper understanding of imperialism, with respect to the form it has come to take, and what it has come to mean, in our present-day world. The liberal view is incapable of sensing that different historical forces, because they provide both the conditions and the rationales for different types of state expansion, could converge differentially to make some expansions, while similar, appear falsely different; and others, while different, appear falsely similar. Of the two, the liberals err commonly on the latter.

The liberal view of imperialism is historico-analytically blunt. As we understand it, it cannot make the sharp distinction necessary between an antediluvian expansion of a state for the purpose of dominating another and a similar expansion in our time, or any other time in between. It is, therefore, not a historical analysis that the liberal view of imperialism offers us but a wishful *orbiter dictum*.[14] To substantiate this conclusion let us take a detailed look at the most recent and daring restatement of the liberal line by Benjamin Cohen.[15]

The Liberal False Claim to Ethical Neutrality

Cohen's main reason for taking up the subject, "The basic question of imperialism," was that there exists a multiplicity of meanings of the word imperialism. His aim was to find a "more appropriate procedure [that] would retain the term, but [would] attempt to give it a well-defined meaning, ethically neutral and objective, [and] that would make it useful for analysis of political economy of international relations."[16]

Such being the chosen burden of the book, the minds of readers would be alerted most keenly to the *appropriate procedure* that Cohen would fashion to accomplish his objective. Different readers will look for different things in the procedure. Those readers who understand political economy of international relations inadequately to mean not more than the slapping together of politics and economics for the purpose of explaining social stability, the absence of war, and the presence of economic growth would like to see Cohen neutralize the term imperialism and link it to the explanation of war and economic growth. And those readers who understand political economy to mean no less than the historical and sociological underpinnings of particular modes of production and the probable potential sources of change in these modes will be bothered less by the "ethical neutrality and objectivity" resultant of Cohen's procedure than by the *honest* compatibility that this procedure can establish between the concept *imperialism* and the real contents of specific histories, in the dual terms of their fixities and their changeabilities.[17] This latter interest, of course, will pay particular attention to *how* Cohen proceeds to assemble the *reasons* constituting his procedure.

Anyone falling within the first group of readers ought to be satisfied with Cohen's treatment of the subject; but anyone who falls in the second group of readers will find Cohen's procedure a colossal disappointment. His appreciation of what is wrong with existing explanations and definitions of imperialism is not superior to his purportedly new offerings. The redeeming quality of this work is perhaps that it is the latest contribution by a liberal which attempts to approach the concept imperialism through some analytic exertions, and thereby tries to incorporate contemporary theories of *inequality* and *dependency* into the understanding of imperialism, thus attempting to update the concept for contemporary usage. Cohen's procedure, however, yields an imperialism that is both political in form and in intent. For this reason, the relationships he establishes between this political phenomenon and dependency and inequality are unconvincing for their wide evasions of the basic causes of contemporary realities and the relevant debates they engender.[18]

This work begins with an exposition of the changes which have occurred in the meaning of the term imperialism. He says that towards the end of the *nineteenth* century, the term was equivalent to colonialism, "the establishment and extension of the political sovereignty of one nation over alien peoples and territories,"[19] and "at the close of the century the term specifically reserved for colonialism of the *maritime* powers — the extension of political sovereignty *overseas*, first by the Portuguese and Spaniards, then by the British, French and the other Europeans, and finally by the Americans and the Japanese."[20] After the turn of the century, critics of capitalism, whom Cohen refers to as "radical liberal," like the Englishman, John Hobson, and Marxists, like Rosa Luxemburg, Rudolf Hilferding, and V.I. Lenin, forced the emphasis to shift "from straight-forward political relationships to more subtle economic forces and motivations — from simple colonialism to more complex forms of economic penetration and domination of markets, sources of supply and investment outlets."[21]

As can be seen from the above, Cohen's principal objections to the prevailing use of the term are its change of meaning from the colonization of one nation by another to colonization of the overseas kind, and the shift in meaning from "straight-forward political relationships" to the "more subtle economic forces and motivations." Taking the two objections together, it is clear that Cohen's critical proposition is that imperialism covers both overland and overseas political relations in the establishment and the extension of political sovereignty over alien peoples and territories. The procedure, Cohen promised, is constructed from a set of reasons which purport to show how wrong it was for the meaning of imperialism to have shifted from a straightforward political relationship to what he calls more subtle economic forces and motivations, seen only in their overseas contexts.

The purpose here is to show that Cohen's procedure denies the concept "imperialism," a living historical concept, the precise historical specificity which is needed to account for the subtle variations within the concept's essential meaning, and which it needs, in the first place, if it is to have any analytic value at all. The aim here is to show that, once the *proper historical context* is admitted, the basic problem ceases to be why the meaning is confined to overseas expansion of political sovereignty, or why the meaning shifted "unaccountably" from the political to the economic. The basic problem becomes that imperialism is wrongly used to refer to particular international events during a particular phase within what we consider the proper historical specificity; or that it is used improperly to refer to imprecise relationships which are trans-epochal and, therefore, historico-analytically useless, because of their very imprecision.

Our position has been that historic specificity is indispensable for the definition of imperialism by virtue of the fact that it is a historical concept. And for this reason, we find the basic flaw in Cohen's position to be its historic imprecision with respect to the proper historical specificity which must attend this historical concept. We also find a basic flaw in the views of those Cohen refers to as the "radical liberals," but the flaw is not that these writers shifted the meaning of imperialism from the political to the economic. The flaw is their contextual over-precision within the proper historic specificity. These two flaws have a common root which we have described as Eurocentric.

We intend to show that, at bottom, Cohen's procedure is nothing more than a carefully poised confrontation between a political Eurocentric *imprecision* and an economic Eurocentric *over-precision*; and that Cohen's procedure consists of no more than reasons why the confrontation should be resolved in favour of the former.

We noted earlier that one of Cohen's main objections to the use of the term imperialism was that at the close of the nineteenth century it had come to be reserved for "colonialism of the *maritime* powers — the extension of political sovereignty *overseas*." This objection can be easily sustained, for, whatever the term may or may not mean, reserving its use for "overseas extensions" alone allows the equally important "overland extension" to escape the imperialist tag. There are, however, Eurocentric explanations for the use of the term, as it stood at the close of the century.

One explanation is that the sources of immediate curiosity for European observers of the period, that is, what played consciously on their minds, were not *overland* extensions of sovereignties. This is because they had come to accept the areas of successful overland extensions of European sovereignties — Europe itself, South America, North America, Australia, and New Zealand — as part of an enlarged Europe; and, therefore, they had come to accept the stories of the conquests of these areas as part of European history. To these observers, then, the European "overland" covered all parts of the world where European sovereignties and domination had been successfully extended.

It was for this reason that the observers of the period saw any other extension beyond the successful areas into Africa and Asia as an "overseas" phenomenon. A second explanation is that we must also realize that expansions into Africa and Asia during the late nineteenth century were proving difficult for Europe, for the many reasons which Hobson detailed.[22] In most cases the observers believed wrongly, of course, that the extension of European sovereignty was taking place on the seas in the form of European gunboat parades rather than real extensions into African and Asian lands.

The third explanation is that at the turn of the century the observers could not appreciate the full effects of the earlier successful European expansions; but they could appreciate the massive disruptive impacts which the later waves of European expansion into Africa and Asia made on Europe and on European lives. What, therefore, appeared new to these observers was the apparently more difficult extensions of European sovereignties into Africa and Asia, which they saw, in the improved capitalist conditions of their time, much more clearly in terms of costs and benefits to Europe, and which they sought to understand in terms of the rationality of European expansions of earlier capitalist periods.

However, if we concede the obvious point that practically all the extensions of European sovereignties had to be initiated by sea from Europe proper, then the reservation of the term for "overseas" extension of sovereignty is to be rejected not for the reasons Cohen suggests but for the Eurocentric arrogance which saw the successful extensions of earlier periods as part of Europe and, therefore, justified the reservation of the "overseas" connotation for the efforts to extend European sovereignties into Africa and Asia.

From the Eurocentric view, and for the reasons mentioned above, the difference between the earlier and the later waves of European capitalist expansion appeared falsely, by the turn of the century, as different in kind, rather than as merely a difference composed of differences in times of occurrence and differences in the apparent ease of extending European sovereignties. The main flaw in this conception of imperialism is the insistence on seeing the phenomenon in the restricted terms of extensions of sovereignties, rather than in the more comprehensive terms of the extensive and the intensive *expansion* of European capitalist culture through European domination.[23]

The basic limitation in this Eurocentric view is the curious reluctance to connect and relate the world implications of European expansions prior to the nineteenth century, during that period and onwards, into a coherent singular world-history. When we do not confuse expansion with its political subpart, the extension of sovereignty, this reluctance becomes strange, because it ought to be clear, if only through hindsight, that the European expansion and domination which initiated the modern world-system contained some "evolutionary consistence." Call it natural history, if you like, but it appears convincingly to be a history which has clear origins in the crisis of European feudalism and the need for extra-European inputs to overcome the crisis. In the process, it was not merely the crisis which was overcome; the European economy, European society, and the entire world were transformed. This world-historical process has its dramatic world-historical significance in the colourless dispatch of the first "discovery" ships in the fifteenth century.

If this is so, then, from the world-system perspective, it is impossible to sustain any serious dislocations between the European expansions overseas initiated in the fifteenth century and any subsequent changes in the forms and in the accompanying experiences of this initial expansion. All subsequent events of world-system significance appear to have flowed from this initial cause of the development of the world capitalist system;

and all such events seem to have meanings in the logic of antecedent events during this specific historic epoch. Hindsight is indispensable in understanding this position.

It is for this reason that the world-system perspective would insist that if the term imperialism is reserved for events in a particular portion of this long but specific historic period, then the events which imperialism is supposed to describe must be seen to be *different* in their historic essentials from other events during the entire period of modern history. To the extent that events described by a particular term do not differ from others, the same term should cover the other events. Some functional conditions, however, should be attached to such a general and versatile term. It should be able to capture and account for false similarities and differences in the evolution of the history in which it plays such a vital role.

In approaching a historical concept this way, there must always be a clear end-means context within its historical specificity. Indeed, the end and the means must be seen as inseparably linked, if human thinking and actions which constitute events in history are not to be periodized merely by the convenience of dates, or by what Heilbroner would call *heroic will*, in contrast to what he calls *historic force*.[24] Means may change, but these changes do not necessarily change history, the historic force. History changes, however, thus calling for changes in key concepts when the contextual ends, that is, the *historic theme and motive*, change.

Eurocentric understanding of world-history has tended to focus exclusively on the changing means of European exploitation of the rest of the world for the purpose, the end, of accumulating capital in Europe and away from the rest of the world. It tends to appreciate these changing means principally in terms of their effects in Europe and on European lives. It is for these reasons, that, when the "world-wide" exploitation relations change from such forms as "plunder and incursion" to "bridgehead constructions and trade in 'pacotilles'," and from this to "unequal trade in substance," and finally to "unequal trade under neo-colonialism," Eurocentrics pronounce changes in epochs, stages, phases, etc. No one could doubt the significance of these changes in means and forms, but their significance should lie not in themselves and how they explain the European scene but how they relate to the continuity of the exploitation enterprise, and how they explain the world-system in evolution as it relentlessly pursues its historic theme of capital accumulation and its unequal incidence.

It is for the above reasons that the world-system perspective ought to be clear and, on being clear, should insist that the term imperialism, if it has any relevance at all to the exploitative relations between the Europeanized centre and the sprawling non-European periphery, as it has been created, should not only date from the origins of capitalism in Europe in the fifteenth century, but also that this term's analytic value should lie in its sensitivity to the changing centre-periphery relations with respect to the continuity of the accumulation of capital theme of modern world-history. We readily concede that the *forms*, that the means, of imperialism have changed through its history for many reasons, including the need for the enterprise to up-date its world-wide superstructural legitimization; but we maintain that imperialism, as it describes, or rather stands for, a historic theme, has remained the same in its history, simply because its motive has remained the same.

The other strong objection Cohen raised against the use of the term imperialism was that, after the turn of the century, radical-liberals changed the meaning from political to economic. Surely this change in meaning is understandable by the simple truth of it all that, by that time, the understanding of the dynamics of history had improved enough for it to be appreciated that what, as the "final explanation," may have appeared "political" could have other explanations far too fundamental for the gross, and all-encompassing, term political to capture adequately. This change does help us to understand much better *why* the first Portuguese and Spanish ships sailed the oceans and "discovered" the Americas and the other parts of the world, and as a result changed the entire "unrelated" fact of the history of the world into one of a related and increasingly interdependent whole, world-history. The political view cannot do this. For, couched in terms of *"who gets what, when, how,"*[25] the political cannot relate the basic facts of the *what* in terms which should lead us to pursue the interests and pressures that are the motivating forces in the currents of a particular history. In political analysis, the initial *why* which should inform us on who gets what, when, and how always remains a bothersome evasion.

As before, a closer look at Cohen's objection leads us to a Eurocentric predilection. Rightist or Leftist, Eurocentric liberals tend to avoid confronting the *why* in their politics. This definition is usually applied to national societies, where for them such a confrontation may not be strictly necessary. They tend to take for granted the reasons *why* "who gets what" gets it, "and how" he gets it. Eurocentrics of the liberal persuasion tend to consider it obvious that the answers to the *why* are located in the *nature* of societies, which they understand in terms of societies' superstructural referents called political cultures. They stop there, because if they pursue the matter further they will end up seeing the nature of modern society in its more fundamental terms, and thus end up criticizing capitalism. And this is precisely what they do not want to do. The same is the case for most Leftists. If they confront the initial *why*, they will end up criticizing socialist régimes and this is what they do not want to do.

This reluctance is what accounts for the Eurocentric liberal imprecision in defining imperialism. To avoid confronting the historically specific, which is economic in its essentials, they define imperialism so imprecisely that it can represent intergroup relationships across all ages.[26] This is the only way they can absolve capitalism from the imperialist relations on which it thrives at the world level. At the world level, and within the world-system perspective, however, there is no such thing as the merely political. The political is considered the property of subsystems within the world-system, for analytic purposes; but at the conceptual level, the economic relates to the political (and other things), as cause relates to effect.[27]

All this may be plain enough, but let us elaborate on it some more to conclude the charge that Eurocentric liberals are imprecise in their conception of imperialism. To demonstrate this, we shall critically examine Cohen's conception of imperialism in the light of the construction of his so-called new procedure.

Liberal Eurocentric Imprecision

Cohen states: "Formally speaking, imperialism refers to a relationship." The relationship itself is "international — between nations."[28] From this formal conception, Cohen proceeds to ask this pertinent question: "What kind of international relationship is imperialism about?" He answers the question this way:

Manifestly, it can refer only to a particular subset of relationships. Specifically, imperialism refers to that kind of international relationship characterized by a particular assymetry — the assymetry of *dominance* and *dependence*. Nations are inherently unequal. International inequality is a fact of life ... what is most important about this fact of life is that it frequently ... results in the effective

56

subordination of some nations by others; that is, in the imposition of some sort of rule or control. Here we approach the irreducible core of meaning in the ambiguous word imperialism. Imperialism refers to those particular relationships between inherently unequal nations which involve effective subjugation, the *actual* exercise of influence over behaviour. The concept is basically operational. Inequality is the necessary condition; active affirmation of superiority and inferiority is the logical condition of sufficiency. (Emphases added.)[29]

This quotation is interesting because it brings out the basic flaw in Cohen's procedure to render the term imperialism ethically neutral and analytically precise. The flaw is that his *manifest* conception is *analytically imprecise*, and this is due to the fact that his *specific* conception is historically without a (specific) base, making it historically undiscriminating and, therefore, *historically imprecise*.

We can accept that imperialism refers to a particular subset of relationships. But *precisely* how do we come to know what this "particular subset" is, among the totality of all possible subsets? And *precisely* what relation does this "particular subset" bear with the other subsets in the possible totality, hierarchically and causally, insofar as this particular subset of relationships is able to bring about imperialism, defined as "a sort of rule or control ... between inherently unequal nations which involves effective subjugation, the actual exercise of influence over behaviour." We need to know the clear identity of this particular subset of relationships; and further, we need to know whether this subset remains the same, or whether it changes with changing historical forces. Unless we are clear on these points, we are likely to be led by Cohen into believing that we can change the identities of the particular subset of relationships to suit particular conveniences, or worse, that we can arbitrarily say that this particular subset of relationships has always been one thing or the other. This, in fact, is our cardinal fear.

The above questions are based on the self-evident fact that for a particular subset of relationships to lead to the condition of dominance and dependence for the purpose of effective subjugation, meaning the actual exercise of influence over behaviour, this particular subset must rank in importance above all the other subsets in the totality of relationships. This should be so because not all subsets of relationships can at all times and in all historic circumstances be of equal potency in initiating dominance and dependence to the extent that they can create the social relations and conditions Cohen calls imperialism, the irreducible core meaning of which is the effective subjugation, the actual exercise of influence over behaviour.

The main problem, then, is that the question as to what this particular subset of relationships is, cannot be answered outside clearly defined contexts. These contexts must, of necessity, be historical. That is, they must be set within specific and precise historic forces. It is within such historical contexts that we can locate the specific historical imperatives, within a given historicity, which define the primacy of the particular subset Cohen refers to. And further, it is this location, by way of a historical definition, which suggests the *motivation* that spawns the imperialist dynamic, which rides on the mechanisms of domination and dependence (initiated by inequality) towards the precise end of effective subjugation. The adjective, *effective*, is history-bound. Its meaning is dependent on historic circumstances captured by such things as the levels of technology, size of the "world," the strengths of the states involved in this "world," all relating to the series of differences within the evolution of a given mode of production.

The root of Cohen's problem of imprecision is to be found in his unaccountable omission of the term *expansion* from his specific definition of imperialism.[30] The assymetry of inequality does not unaccountably lead to the assymetries of dominance and dependence. Unless we are prepared to see imperialism as some sort of insanity, which flows out of the mere presence of inequality between units, we are forced to dwell on the precise causes which make expansion a *logical* outcome of inequality, a *rational* act to follow the recognition and appreciation of inequality. Unless we are ready to seek refuge in the mystification that "expansion impulses abhor inequality,"[31] we are forced to pursue the *rational logicalities* which justify expansion, because inequality exists. This rational logicality is to be found in the historical sociology of a particular historical epoch, as it relates to the expanding unit. And this is to be understood in terms of the social pressures which breed and typify the dominant hopes and fears of the expanding units, and, therefore, could be said to define the "needs" of a particular historical epoch. Outside such candid historical specificity, Cohen's procedure cannot provide an "ethically neutral" conception of imperialism. The ethics of the neutrality Cohen seeks are to be found in the honesty and the sensitivity with which they approach and distinguish between differences in historic forces.

Lack of candid historical specificity is a grievous flaw in the analysis of historical concepts. So grievous is this flaw in Cohen's case that even if we accept that imperialism refers to unequal relationships between inherently unequal nations, that inequality is the necessary condition for imperialism, and that the active affirmation of superiority and inferiority is its logical condition of sufficiency, we are still justified in questioning whether "nations" have always been *this* unequal. The question is whether the degrees of inequalities between nations, as we know them today, have always been a fact of "international" life. If not, then what needs to be explained is precisely what Cohen presents to us as the unimpeachable facts of international life.[32] The relevant questions which Cohen's intended new procedure should have addressed, then, are the following: *How* did "nations" come to be "this unequal," when historically they were not "this unequal"? More importantly, *why* was this increasing unequalizing process set in motion? Cohen does not address himself to these questions. He and other liberals do not even allow for their pertinence. By skirting these questions, Cohen's treatment of imperialism does not take into account the origins and the dynamism of the imperialist process in a way that makes it relevant to the understanding of contemporary realities. This is clearly shown in the most unsatisfactory links Cohen attempts to establish between his conception of imperialism and the apologetic and equivocal views he has of *dependency* and *exploitation*.[33]

Why did Cohen not take cognizance of these crucially relevant questions in formulating his general theory of imperialism? The answer must be simply that Cohen, like many other writers of his ideological persuasion, refuses to accept the capitalist culpability for the modern world. Such refusal cannot stand the severe scrutiny which necessarily attends the correct questions, as raised above. This refusal always leads to fuzzy theorizing on imperialism. In Cohen's particular case this refusal led him to formulate, by 1974 expectations, a backward "general theory" of imperialism as the product of "the good old game of power politics [which is inherent in] the structure of the system of nations."[34] This incredibly naïve formulation is not even capable of relating the functional utility of the state, as we know it in modern times, to the development of the capitalist world-system.[35]

This simplistic notion of imperialism is most insecurely based; and Cohen conveniently exposes the foundations of this insecurity very early in the book. He states:

Conceptually, imperialism has to do not only with *form* of dominance, but with the forces giving rise to and maintaining the particular relationship as well. Definitionally, however, imperialism is indifferent as to alternative variations of such forms and forces. For example, given the existence of international inequality and the interactions of specific groups and organizations, imperial control may be imposed directly, through the extension of formal political sovereignty; or it may be accomplished indirectly, through informal diplomatic or military pressures or economic penetration. Likewise, the factors underlying and motivating this control may be something else, such as the pursuit of political power or influence or the securing of strategic outposts. Properly defined for analytical purposes such as ours, imperialism allows for all these potential forms and forces. It simply refers to any relationship of effective domination or control, political or economic, direct or indirect of one nation over another.

This is not meant to suggest that the alternative variations of forms and forces are unimportant.... The problem precisely is this: to determine which forms are the most prevalent, which forces the most potent and what their interconnections really are.[36]

At first glance, this long quote appears to be inspired by an acute case of analytic open-mindedness, for it seems to invite us to see the problem as residing in the proper *determinations* of the *prevalence of forms*, the *potency of forces*, and in the *proper determination* of the *interconnections* between them. Upon closer contextual examination, however, we come to see that Cohen's understanding of *forms* and *forces*, taken together with his understanding of *motives*, pitch the subject's *problématique* at such an irreverently high level of evasive abstraction that it becomes impossible to pursue the subject creatively in terms of any meaningful historical specificity. It becomes impossible to discuss the subject in terms of the "rationality of an age." Emanating from this primary flaw are some critical conceptual, definitional, and analytical misconceptions and impositions, which leave little room, if any at all, for any other view but that imperialism, irrespective of time, that is, irrespective of technological and other differential referents, is primarily a political phenomenon.

The problem is precisely that the "alternative variations of such forms and forces," which are so very crucial for Cohen's thesis, are theoretically, and surreptitiously, resolved in favour of the prevalence of political forms and potency of political forces. Consequently, and most untenably, the principal motivation is made to appear also as political.

The conceptual trick is that, after this, imperialism can only be a political phenomenon, because the particular subset of relationships upon which Cohen hinges his whole theory then turns out to be political. In short, Cohen prejudges the issue, by being fuzzy and *imprecise*.[37]

It is legitimate for Cohen to conceptualize imperialism as having to do with both the form of dominance and the forces giving rise to, and maintaining, *the* particular dominance relationship. But if by *form* Cohen means the direct or indirect (and perhaps even the partial or the impartial) nature of the domination or control, and if by forces he refers to the constellation of *means* for implementing the domination, then we have to ask whether it is proper for Cohen to leave it at that. We have to ask, in the dual spirit of criticism and suggestion, the following question: What of the epochal forces which refer not to means of implementation but to the variations in the crucial interconnection between the varying forms and varying implementing forces? Cohen does not mention these crucial variations because of the historical insensitivity of his procedure.

The variations between the changing forms and the changing implementing forces are the factors which define the motivation of imperialism. Any variation in motivation, in this context, cannot be properly appreciated outside the variations in the interconnection between form and forces. It is not enough for Cohen to say, as he does with respect to motives, that "likewise, the factors underlying and motivating this control may be something else, such as the pursuit of political power or influence or the securing of strategic outposts." Cohen treats *motivation*, one of the keys to historical specificity, very poorly in his constructions. This shows very clearly in his crucially placed statement that imperialism allows, for analytic purposes, all the potential (possible?) forms and forces. This is evasion of the most prominent kind. The variations in the interconnection are lost, and so far lost that in epitomizing the essentials of imperialism Cohen leaves out motivation entirely. He says imperialism "simply refers to any relationship of effective domination or control, political or economic, directly or indirectly of one nation over another." In this, the forces of implementation have been made deceptively to appear as the forces which create motivation.

Cohen's procedure is based on the conceptual presentation of two bags, one containing forms of imperialism and the other containing forces for implementing imperialism; and upon some reflection (or is it after some hesitation?) one more bag is added to contain motives of imperialism. We are then told that the real analytic problem lies in matching the

61

prevalence of forms with the potency of implementing forces. The unanswered question is this: For what purpose are we indulging in this matching exercise? Cohen should have stated explicitly that this exercise is meant to identify the changes in underlying motives of domination. Unfortunately, he omits to state it. And for this omission, one is at a loss as to how Cohen can claim to be dealing with a theory of imperialism, when the very dynamic element in his procedure, motivation, which we believe is constant for capitalist world-history, is ignored.

Cohen's aim in his book was to find an appropriate procedure that would render the term imperialism ethically neutral and objective for the proper analysis of the political economy of international relations. This is a laudable aim. But by failing to make the vital distinction between forces of implementation and the historically specific forces of motivation, Cohen's procedure could only conclude on the backward and mystifying notion that imperialism "... is ... not so much the ability as the 'ought compulsion'"[38] as it pertains to the political imperatives in the structure of the system of nations.

This effort does not deserve the grandiose name theory. In its terms, the "ought compulsion" in world-history — the conscious and methodical process of capital accumulation — is entirely lost, and with it the roles of the peoples in those parts of the world which have borne by far the larger part of the losses in the accumulation of capital enterprise from its beginnings till the present.

It would have been useless, for our purpose, to have discussed the liberal conception of imperialism at such length, if it were not for the fact that the liberal conception, even in its simplicity, manages to alert us to the fact that, although imperialism is defined in terms of state expansionism, in the context of the structure of the relationships between states, the immediate cause of state expansion does not appear to reside in the state, as an abstract entity, but rather in *specific interests* within the individual state apparatus which cohere into a motivation; and further, that it is the conflict between these interests in the interstate system which leads to war.

We do not approach imperialism merely as a bothersome war-causing phenomenon but as a world-historical phenomenon, with certain clear and specific implications which may include wars. This means that we can reject such things as the war-loving connotation attached to this interest by Schumpeter, and Cohen's naïve re-statement of the conventional wisdom that imperialism is caused by war-prone politics among states, without necessarily having to reject the important pointers to the proper identity of the specific interests within, and between, states which lead them to want to expand. What is left unconsidered by the liberal view is the proper context, defined in terms of historic forces, for the discussion of these interests. It is in this regard that the radical conception of imperialism, which Hobson initiated, appears attractive because it promises to be superior.

Notes

1. Joseph A. Schumpeter, "On Imperialism," in Kenneth E. Boulding and Tapan Mukerjee, eds., *Economic Imperialism* (University of Michigan Press, Ann Arbor, Mich., 1972), pp. 34–59.
2. Joseph A. Schumpeter, *Imperialism and Social Classes* (Augustus M. Kelly Publishers, New York, 1951), p. 89.
3. The other terms have connotations very different from "unlimited."
4. Schumpeter (see note 2 above), p. 59.
5. Schumpeter (see note 2 above), p. 39.
6. Schumpeter (see note 2 above), p. 39.
7. E.M. Winslow, *The Pattern of Imperialism: A Study in Theories of Power* (Octagon Press, New York, 1972); Hannah Arendt, *Imperialism: The Origins of Totalitarianism* (Allen and Unwin, London, 1968); the essays by Richard Koebner, "The Concept of Economic Imperialism," D.K. Fieldhouse, "Imperialism: An Historiographical Revision," David S. Landes, "The Nature of Economic Imperialism," all reprinted in Boulding and Mukerjee (see note 1 above).
8. Winslow (see note 7 above), pp. 215–216.
9. Landes (see note 7 above), p. 141.
10. Benjamin J. Cohen, *The Question of Imperialism: The Political Economy of Dominance and Dependence* (Macmillan, London, 1974), p. 245.
11. J. Strachey, *The End of Empire* (Gollancz, London, 1959).
12. Harry Magdoff, *The Age of Imperialism* (Monthly Review Press, New York, 1969), p. 13.
13. The concern for war, for different reasons, cuts across liberal, radical, and Marxist lines of thought. We shall refer to them at appropriate points in this volume.
14. Joseph Frankel, a liberal, in a recent essay, seems to think highly of Cohen's work for what appear to be the same reasons why we criticize him. See his "A Double Omission: A Reply to Dr. Kubalkova and Professor Cruickshank," *British Journal of International Studies* 4, no. 1 (1978): 61.
15. We ignore Cohen's claim in the introduction of his book that he is neither wholly a liberal, nor a radical. We consider his work a good example of the liberal line of argument.
16. Cohen (see note 10 above), p. 10.
17. See Robert Nisbet, *Social Change and History: Aspects of the Western Theory of Development* (Oxford University Press, London, 1969), for the distinctions made here.
18. See my "The New International Economic Order and Imperialism: A Context for Evaluation," *Proceedings of IPRA Seventh General Conference* (1979), pp. 194–215.

19. Cohen (see note 10 above), p. 10.
20. Cohen (see note 10 above), p. 10.
21. Cohen (see note 10 above), p. 11.
22. See John A. Hobson, *Imperialism: A Study* (Allen and Unwin, London, 1965).
23. This is a critical point. The mere extension of sovereignties is not enough to represent the phenomenon in its total complexities.
24. See Robert L. Heilbroner, *The Future as History: The Historic Currents of Our Time and the Direction in which They are Taking America* (Grove Press, New York, 1961), p. 28, where he depicts social history as "no longer heroic will, but historic force." See also his *An Inquiry into the Human Prospect* (Calder and Boyars, London, 1975), and Pablo Gonzales Casanova, "Historical Systems and Social Systems," *Studies in Comparative International Development* 8, no. 2 (1973): 227–246.
25. Harold D. Lasswell, *Politics: Who Gets What, When, How* (MacGraw-Hill, New York, 1936). Cohen is clearly influenced by this definition of politics.
26. Or, like the other Eurocentrics, they define capitalism as if it dropped from the European sky in the nineteenth century.
27. I. Wallerstein's work on *The Modern World-System: Capitalist Agriculture and the Origins of European World Economy in the Sixteenth Century* (Academic Press, New York, 1976), makes this point much clearer. See later discussion and other references.
28. Cohen (see note 10 above), p. 13. He goes on to ask: "But What Is a Nation?" We shall not get very far if we pause to take Cohen up on this inclusion of nations as the units in imperialist relationships. Surely it should be very clear that some of the relationships we should call imperialistic did not exist between nations as we have come to know them today. We shall therefore read the above formal definition of imperialism as a relationship between groups of people, whether they appear as nations or not. The question, as put by Cohen, is interesting at this level of analysis only if he is prepared to argue that the *nation* is different from the *state* and together they connote something different from the *nation-state*; and further that it is the state which causes the nation in imperialist ventures; and furthermore, that, at this level of analysis, the state itself is a product and an instrument of the development of the capitalist history itself. See my "Approaching the Peculiarity of the Caribbean Plight within the Paradox of the Representative State in the Contemporary World-System" (Research paper, United Nations University, Tokyo, 1980).
29. Cohen (see note 10 above), pp. 14–15.
30. Landes (see note 7 above), p. 141.
31. This will be no improvement on Landes' "vacuum" analogy cited in note 9 and referred to again in note 30 above.
32. This leads straight into what we mean by the difference between "small" and "large" states. See my "Caribbean Plight" (note 28 above); and my "Caribbean Prospects for the 1980s: The Plight and the Destiny," in D. Pollock and A. Ritter, eds., *What Kind of Development?* vol. 3 (Carleton University, Ottawa, 1980), pp. 1–51.
33. Cohen (see note 10 above), pp. 233–234.
34. See note 28 above.
35. Cohen (see note 10 above), pp. 15–16.
36. The careful reader of the above long quote will notice that Cohen, by the structure of his sentences, in particular by his use of the words *directly* and *indirectly*, and by the sequence in which he mentions the possible subsets of relationships, leaves no room whatsoever for any other view than the *political*.
37. Cohen (see note 10 above), p. 210.

Chapter Four

The Radical Conception of Imperialism

Hobson's Radical Legacy

A large part of the radical concern with imperialism also deals with the revulsion for the wars which come with state expansions. They differ from the liberals, however, in that in expressing themselves on state expansions and their concomitant wars, they attribute imperialism to specific economic and associated capitalist superstructural interests within the capitalist state. This position derives from the classical radical writer on the subject, John Hobson. Hobson held that the taproot of imperialism was economic: "It is this economic condition of affairs [underconsumption] that forms the taproot of imperialism."[1] However, and strangely, Hobson finds the economic causes of imperialism not in capitalism as an economic form, but in the specific interests of a class of individuals within the capitalist state. As he puts it: "The driving force of class interest which stimulates and supports this false economy we have explained.... It is idle to attack Imperialism or Militarism as political expedients or policies unless the axe is laid at the economic root of the tree, and the classes for whose interest Imperialism works are shorn of the surplus revenues which seek this outlet."[2]

This class of individuals is defined by capitalist financial interest, by the fact that they stand to amass capitalist gains in the form of higher returns on their investments, after the state has expanded as well as in the course of the expansion process itself. To the radical, there is nothing about capitalism which ought to propel its state irresistibly towards *unlimited* expansion, as had occurred with Britain between 1870 and the 1900s. Such *extra* expansion as Britain had indulged in beyond the *required limit*, during the late nineteenth century, had been the result of policy tricks played by the few who stood to gain by their use of the state apparatus, at the expense of the many within Britain.

To the radical, then, while the motive of imperialism is economic, in the restricted sense of economic class interest of the few capitalist financiers, it is linked with the political in that it is through the political medium that these few financiers have ample opportunities to get the state, and the public, to adopt and pursue expansionist policies beyond the *acceptable limit*. From the radical perspective, then, the motive of imperialism, understood to mean an extended state expansion beyond a *limit*, is economic in nature, but the kinetic factor underlying the motive is political, a policy adopted, or condoned by the state.

Hobson wrote his classic on the European scene generally, but he was particularly concerned with his native Great Britain. He was unhappy with the *irrational* untidiness of the British scene, which he blamed on expansionist resource-consuming wars in search of *unnecessary* markets. His views were opposed to many of his time, but more so to those of the arch-imperialist Cecil Rhodes. Hobson reasoned that the foreign markets for which the expansionist wars were fought, during the late nineteenth century, appeared necessary for the wrong reasons. He did not see the problem as a need for markets. He saw it as a problem of underconsumption, caused by the fact that the workers were paid so little by the capitalists that the workers were unable to purchase all that was produced. Therefore, in order to get rid of the resulting excess production, capitalists then projected the need for external markets, and the waging of expansionist wars towards this end, as both logical and rational. Hobson's opposing view was this: Whatever was produced could be consumed, for if the capitalist were to pay the workers enough to purchase all that was produced in Britain, then there would be no over-production problem, and consequently no need to waste precious British resources in expansionist wars beyond the *necessary limit*.

This book by Hobson, *Imperialism: A Study*, is very complex. There was no part of British or European social life, during the period, insofar as it was relevant to explain imperialism, as he understood it, that he did not eloquently touch upon. He found it criminally obnoxious that not only were precious resources being squandered to the primary benefit of a few financiers in expansionist wars, but also that beyond the *admissible* extension of the state, the lives of the imperialized peoples, who tended to resist being permanently crushed, were being interfered with to no ostensible good. Such wars could not help either the European civilization or the imperialized peoples.

The question which bothered Hobson was this: What was to be done with the imperialized races, whose lives, lands, and cultures had been exposed to Western civilization through the activities of an unruly bunch of capitalist agents, such as explorers, prospectors, adventurers, and adventurous traders? Hobson's response was that Britain, the hegemonic power of the time, was over-extended in the state-expansion business. For this reason, other European powers should be given their chances to expand their states, too. The persistent British entrenchment and further involvement in this enterprise only aroused the jealousies of other European powers and led to ugly scenes between European powers, outside their continent.

He argued forcefully that, since at that time the doctrine of free trade was in vogue, no one European nation could monopolize any new trade that resulted from state expansion. He believed that benefits from state expansions were, in the final analysis, shared by all "civilized" nations; and for this reason European nations should approach the control and exploitation of those newly opened-up distant lands in the spirit of *internationalism*.

This point of view had much appeal for Hobson because he reasoned, rightly, that it was too idle to consider that the white Western nations would abandon their interests in those "new" lands and their peoples. Hobson liked this internationalist prescription because he believed it would accomplish the following: It would distribute the cost of imperialism fairly among European nations, and thus significantly relieve Britain, the most extended nation in the imperialist business at the time; it would remove jealousies and wars among European powers; and internationalism would guarantee the maximum protection of the peoples of the imperialized races.

The above is our understanding, in a narrative way, of Hobson's general views on imperialism. These views are not against state expansion. They merely caution against *excessive* state expansion. It was mainly the costs involved in state expansion, *beyond* a limit and in ways which could be *justified*, that Hobson condemned. The firm position which Hobson has handed down to other radicals on the subject and around which their differences revolve is this: *State expansionist policies ought to be limited and they must not lead to war.*

Hobson's argument on imperialism can be described as being period specific because his treatment of the subject is situated within a definite time period, the late nineteenth century, and its relevance is similarly time-bound. *Period specificity*, however, could differ from *historic specificity* because the period need not coincide with the entire duration of a specific history. This distinction is of great interest to us in pursuing the continuity of imperialism thesis and for advancing the Eurocentric charge. Towards this end, we need to take a much closer look at Hobson's arguments. To do this properly, we need to sail very close to Hobson's definitional premises.

It might prove helpful if we keep it firmly in mind that Hobson's position differs from ours on many points, but principally for the following two reasons.

First, since he identifies imperialism so closely with capitalist financial interests, it is not possible, within his framework, to consider state expansions which occurred before the clear emergence of this clearly defined class of individuals as imperialist. The close association which Hobson established between imperialism and the political opportunities available to capitalist financiers, therefore, makes his conception of imperialism historically *over-precise*. Certainly Hobson's view is that state expansions during the earlier phases of the capitalist formation do not qualify to be called imperialist.

Second, both the context in which he situates his case against "underconsumption" and the social referents with which he argues his case against the unlimited state expansion of the late nineteenth century constitute a clear case of Eurocentricity, in that they appear to have meaning and make sense only in the European circumstances of the time. Hobson's treatment of European interests in this connection is a good example of the Eurocentric presentation of hegemonic history as larger than European history, and European history as larger than world-history. In fact, he ignores world-history all through his discourse on imperialism.

A Close and Critical Look at Hobson's Legacy

Hobson begins his study with the warning that imperialism, like any other "ism," is difficult to define; and for this reason the recognition of a certain broad consistency in the term's relation to other kindred terms is perhaps the best way to begin. I agree. He selects *nationalism, internationalism*, and *colonialism* as *imperialism's* "three closest congeners," each in itself no less elusive to pin down.[3]

It is difficult to proceed beyond the first page of this work without wondering why Hobson did not include *capitalism* in the selected kindred terms. One is quickly alerted to the fact that the *over-precise* nature of Hobson's choice of the relevance of past history is responsible for this omission. His subject was the so-called "modern imperialism" of the late nineteenth century. To treat the subject, Hobson took for granted the capitalist reality of the time, but he ignored its relevant past. As a Eurocentric, he did not have to specify the "world" involvement in the origin and in the evolution of the economic conditions of the phenomenon he defines. Had he done this, however, it would have helped him in establishing any continuities and variations which attended the phenomenon over a longer historical period.

Giovanni Arrighi is right when he says that "after all, Hobson's theory is famous precisely for the connection that it establishes between 'imperialism' and 'capitalism'; and this link is indeed its peculiar and original feature";[4] and that for Hobson, the link between "imperialism" and "capitalism" was "so obvious that it could be passed over in silence or condensed into a few introductory pages and scattered remarks."[5] This is true, and because of this very truth, it is legitimate to ask the following questions: (1) By taking this vital connection for granted, has Hobson not become the prisoner of his own over-precise historical specificity? (2) By becoming such a prisoner, has Hobson not ignored crucial similarities between earlier and later forms of the imperialist phenomenon? (3) Because of this, did Hobson not make too much of *apparent* differences between the "three closest congeners" and imperialism, in the cause of establishing the latter's identity?

These questions are important, for in handling historical concepts, one is not at liberty to claim an *unjustified* period specificity. The reasons for choosing a specific period must be clearly stated and they must be open to discussion on the precise historic identity of the period. The choice of historical watersheds must have reasons behind it. Hobson is blind to similarities between the periods before and after his 1870 baseline, because his reasons were Eurocentric; and, accordingly, his treatment of imperialism is Eurocentric. It is in conflict with, or at the very least it differs from, our conception of imperialism as an increasingly world-wide phenomenon, seen centrally as the expansion of capitalism and the increasing accumulation of capital on a "world" scale.

Hobson asserts that nationalism was the vogue in the nineteenth century and that it was the debasement of genuine nationalism that led nationalism to overflow "its natural banks and absorb ... territories of reluctant and unassimilable peoples"; and further that it is this that marked "the passage from nationalism to spurious colonialism on the one hand, and imperialism on the other."[6] He defines colonialism as

> consisting in the migration of part of a nation to vacant or sparsely peopled foreign lands, the emigrants carrying with them full rights of citizenship in the mother country, or else establishing local self-government in close conformity with her institutions and under her final control, may be considered a genuine expression of nationality, a territorial enlargement of the stock, language and institutions of a nation.[7]

The definition of imperialism is obliquely approached in these words: "Either [nations] have severed the connection and set up for themselves separate nationalities, or they have been kept in complete political bondage so far as all major processes of government are concerned, a condition to which the term imperialism is at least as appropriate as colonialism."[8] Australia and Canada were singled out as the only good examples of colonialism; the Cape Colony and Natal, in South Africa, were considered spurious colonialism; and by inference, all other British possessions at the time (1900), were considered as governed by imperialism.[9]

Hobson's entire treatise on imperialism centres on two propositions. The first is that nationalism became perverted somehow, so that instead of producing what he called genuine colonialism, it produced spurious colonialism and imperialism. The second is that from his definitional premises, Hobson portrays genuine colonialism as "good" in contrast to imperialism, which he considers as "bad."

If we take propositions to be statements which can be taken to be *more or less true* for the purpose of validating a much more important matter, then any serious discussion of Hobson's work on this subject ought to try to examine the extent to which it agrees with the validity of Hobson's propositions. In our case, our inquiring reactions to the first proposition are: What caused this "perversion"? Did changes in historic forces have anything to do with it? If so, can Hobson's argument alert us to this? Our reactions to the second proposition are: How solid is the contrast which

Hobson established between colonialism and imperialism? Is colonialism, *à la* Hobson, really different in the contrasting sense from imperialism, *à la* Hobson?

It is always dangerous when defining imperialism to seek the etymological roots of the term in the ancient meaning of the term empire. It invariably leads to historically imprecise definitions of imperialism. Hobson states that "the root idea of empire in the ancient and medieval world was that of a federation of states, under a hegemony, covering in general terms the entire known recognized world, such as was held by Rome under the so-called *pax Romana*."[10] Imperialism in those days, Hobson says, "contained a genuine element of internationalism."[11]

What seems to have bothered Hobson most was that the "triumph of nationalism seem(ed) to have crushed the rising hope of internationalism."[12] He believed this should not have been so because, as the history of *pax Romana* showed, nationalism should be "the plain highway to internationalism."[13]

Hobson approached his worry in the right way. He reasoned that if nationalism manifested divergence, we may suspect a *perversion* of its nature and purpose.[14] Such a perversion, he tells us, is "imperialism, in which nations trespassing beyond the limits of facile assimilation, transform the wholesale stimulative rivalry of varied national types into the *cutthroat struggle of competing empires*." (Emphases added.)[15] This is the rub of Hobson's concern. If nationalism has been perverted from its Roman purity in *nature* and in *purpose* into the British imperialism of the nineteenth century, where instead of nationalism limiting itself to the *real* assimilation of non-national types, we are entitled to know what caused this perversion. The answer must be explained in terms of the fundamental differences between the *nature* and the *purpose* of *pax Romana* and *pax Britannica*.

Having cast the problem in terms of this very loose historical difference, one would have expected Hobson to establish some honest compatibility between historical periodization and changes in historic forces and motives. Hobson does not do so because such was not his intention. Having situated imperialism in this historically imprecise context, Hobson leaves it there and retreats into a historically over-precise context to consider why white civilization of the late nineteenth century dared to do what the Roman civilization dared not do in antiquity!

The Flaw of an Imprecise Solution for an Over-precise Problem

Hobson offered two avenues for the negation of the "modern" imperialism he disliked so much. The first was the multiple radical surgery of laying the axe at the economic root of the imperialist tree so that the classes in whose interest imperialism worked would be shorn of the surplus capital, which sought outlets in imperialism. The second avenue was the reinstitution of the internationalism of antiquity in the late nineteenth century under British hegemony.

On the first avenue for negation, this question is in order. If the taproot of imperialism is presented as the capitalist class interest within imperialist states, once the axe is laid at this economic root, could what would be left be called capitalism? This question implies the more fundamental question of whether there can be capitalism without *capitalists*. Once European capitalists of the late nineteenth century and their surplus revenues were separated, Europe would have had either "socialism" or a return to an earlier phase of capitalist development. In the first case, the historic motive would have changed; and in the second, there would have been a return of earlier ways of pursuing the same capitalist motive of accumulating capital. Neither of these two probabilities excludes imperialism, as Hobson understood it.

As Hobson's own analogy suggests, capitalist class interests do have functions. They initiate and nourish the phenomenon of *capital accumulation*. When one remembers that capital accumulation began to acquire its relevant historical specificity from the fifteenth century, and that the state, its creation and expansion, is a product of capital accumulation, it becomes obvious that Hobson has been far too arbitrary with the chosen historical period for his definition and study of imperialism. By arbitrary, we mean the reason for his chosen time referents for the study of imperialism slights, or ignores, crucial similarities with earlier periods. It magnifies differences which would have paled in significance had the similarities he ignored been considered. In other words, Hobson tampered with the continuity of the capitalist imperialist experience in world-history.

On the second solution of imitating Roman internationalism, Hobson's nostalgia for "golden age" myths got the better of him. It must have been, as Hobson was pondering a solution to the problem, as he formulated it, that his nostalgia for the "peaceful," "even-costed," and "undamaging" exploitation of the "lower" races during the Roman times was aroused. He located the difference between *pax Britannica* and *pax Romana* in the presence of internationalism in the latter. Internationalism meant to Hobson a hierarchical structure of civilized nations, under a single hegemony for the peaceful, efficient, and minimally damaging exploitation of the "lower" races and their lands. Hobson's arguments, taken within their own over-precise terms of reference, may appear impeccable. But they have some severe limitation brought about by a fundamental confusion in Hobson's mind.

He saw the imperialism of the nineteenth century as a European problem; in fact, he saw imperialism as a nineteenth-century European economic (industrial) problem. And yet, in seeking a solution to this over-precisely situated problem, Hobson takes his cue from the "golden age" myths of a distinct, and clearly different, historic past, the Roman era. The limitation, therefore, is one of not understanding the historic identity of the problem he was dealing with, and so much so that he committed the fallacy of recommending a historically imprecise solution to a historically different, but over-precisely stated, problem.

This is the case, for if Hobson was impressed by the state expansion of the Roman era and wanted to know why state expansion of the nineteenth-century era was different, a perversion of nationalism to be precise, so that he could prescribe better ways towards emulating the Romans, then he was compelled by the logic of his own chosen burden to ask in what cogent and specific terms he could have cast, or described, the fundamental differences between the natures and the purposes of the two types of state expansions, the "cutthroat" competition characteristic of the nineteenth century and the "peaceful" state expansion of the Roman era. Had Hobson done this, he would have realized that there was as much in common between European state expansions from the late fifteenth century to the late nineteenth century, irrespective of which nations were the hegemonic powers, as there was very little in common between Roman state expansion and the sixteenth to nineteenth century European state expansions.

We contend that had Hobson done this he would have stumbled over the continuity of imperialism thesis.

If such an approach is adopted, we are led to the *taproot* of imperialism in more fundamental economic terms than Hobson presented them. We will find that we will have to cast the differences in terms of differences in modes of production: differences in production relations, the importance and the necessity of markets, the meanings of wealth, the meanings and the roles of capital, the levels of and the rates of changes in technology, and the differences in the strength of the state, among other things.[16]

From our perspective, it is not admissible that one can discuss state expansion of the nineteenth-century type in any form, especially in the comparative form in which Hobson posed the burden, without explicitly confronting the identity of capitalism in its evolutionary terms and around the categories listed above. The point is that while *pax Romana* "internationalist" state expansion was not capitalist, state expansion of European and other states since the fifteenth century to the present has been capitalist in its inspirations and intents; and as such inextricably related to the accumulation of capital on the "world" scale. Merely by recognizing the arguments above, the continuity of capitalist imperialism becomes "obvious."

Hobson's work is considered *radical* because he tried to see the problem of imperialism in terms of its economic root causes. But his treatment of the subject is not all it could have been because he did not go deep enough into the *roots* of it. He belittled the world implication of the capitalist economic system for the modern imperialism he sought to study. This was inevitable, so long as Hobson did not choose the proper historical context. The modern imperialism of Hobson's time had nothing in common with ancient imperialism of the Roman type, except in appearances. The causes of the "cutthroat" identity of state expansion in his time could not be explained adequately in terms of capitalism's ideological, and other superstructural, referents.[17]

It is impossible to have capitalism at any of its stages without "capitalists" who did not exaggerate the importance of state expansion for their own gains, and who do not try very hard, at the very least, to represent their interests as those of the state. Even more appropriate to our point of view, since there has never been a time since the sixteenth century (at least) when budding capitalists and/or full-fledged capitalists have not sought to control the state and the nation in their interests, it is clearly misleading for Hobson to think that we can abolish the excesses involved in capitalist state expansion by simply wishing away capitalist financiers, while we leave the capitalist system itself intact.

Hobson, a self-proclaimed activist, should have thought the problem through to its real root cause: the unquestioned fetish of incessant capital accumulation, either by private capitalists or by state capitalists, dating from the fifteenth century. For the above reasons alone, if for none others, we feel justified in believing that Hobson's theory is famous for the wrong reasons. Unlike Giovanni Arrighi, we believe that if Hobson's theory of imperialism "is famous precisely for the connection that it establishes between 'imperialism' and 'capitalism'; and [that] this link is indeed its peculiar and original feature,"[18] then the theory is famous for the wrong reasons: the historically *imprecise* search for a solution to a historically *over-precise* problem.

The Flaw of False Eurocentric Contrasts

Hobson was not against the exploitation of the imperialized territories; in fact, as we have indicated above, he held that the domination and the exploitation of these areas were inevitable. His worry was how this could be done as efficiently and with as little interference with the aborigines as possible, so that this inevitable exploitation would cause the minimum of damage to the European civilization of the time.

All through the book, Hobson's argument seems to be that assimilation seemed possible only through white settlement and, therefore, the minimum of justified reason for imperialist annexation should be genuine settlement.[19] This is in accord with Hobson's argument, for he believed that settlement of a European stock in individual colonies would not lead to inter-European rivalries through the development of separate nationalisms, as was the case in South Africa. It would not permit the development of self-conscious nationalism among the natives, since settlement implies the lack of native preponderance.[20] But, then, where such preponderance approached the condition of genuine colonization, Hobson was fully aware that "it has commonly implied the extermination of the lower races, either by war or by private slaughter, as in the case of Australian Bushmen, African Bushmen, and Hottentots, Red Indians, and Maoris, or by forcing upon them the habits of a civilization equally destructive of them."[21]

From the above, we can infer that, principally, it was the apparent difficulty of making Australia or Canada, or even the United States, out of the vast remaining British possession that led Hobson to make the distinction he made between colonialism and imperialism. This appears to be what encouraged him to take such a negative view of the latter. If we agree that the making of North America and Oceania was in the interests of the hegemonic powers and Europe, in the course of capital accumulation, then it becomes clear that the real question which Hobson sought to answer was not as he made it appear, namely, why nationalism had been perverted into imperialism, but rather why what appeared to him to have been a relatively peaceful and cheap accumulation of capital in Britain and Europe, during the earlier periods of the accumulation process (sixteenth to early nineteenth century), had turned sour by the late nineteenth century, by being caught in a "cutthroat struggle" among European nations, and therefore had become expensive for the hegemonic power in particular and for Europe as a whole.[22] Thus, we see that Hobson failed to realize the true nature of the problem he was dealing with in its fundamental terms. He took the development of capitalism and its world-wide imperative too much for granted.

As Adam Smith before him, Hobson's real message was to tell his countrymen, and the Europe of his time, that conditions for efficient accumulation of capital had changed and it was therefore necessary for the accumulators to see the means of accumulation in the new light of changed conditions. He sought to warn them against approaching changed conditions from the route of past means.

This was Hobson's message, as I interpret it:

The accumulation business is getting tougher and tougher all the time. The only way to counteract the diminishing returns which have clearly come into play lately is for Britain to lead the adoption of internationalism. Just as the Romans led the exploitations of their times, never mind the differences between the times, Britain should do the same today. All we need do is keep our financiers in check. We know very well what they are like. They will stop at nothing. Even if to make a shilling, they will not hesitate to let their kith and kin languish in misery in England or, worse, send them to sweat it out in disease-infested Africa.

Let's face it, we cannot make a genuine colonial business out of any part of Africa and Asia. Their climate does not suit us.

They are too uncivilized for us to mix with beyond the minimum contact, if we know what is good for us. We should never forget that we can consume all we produce. It is an economic lie that we *need* to sell to them. Not more than a few of us Europeans need set foot in Africa or Asia to get from the wretched lot what we need to maintain, and advance, our civilization.

All they have is ours. And we can tap all they have for practically nothing, if only we will adopt internationalism. It is sad to admit it, perhaps for some apostles of imperialism among us, but Africa can never be a permanent home for us, and for our civilization. If God wanted us to live there he would have made the climate hospitable to us and the people civilizable and not so preponderant.

Take it from me. I have been there. I have seen the Boer war! To think that members of the highest civilization man has ever seen chose to make a spectacle of themselves by cutting each others throats before the lowest civilization imaginable!

All this wastage of precious European lives and precious European resources could be avoided in future, if only the British governments would stop listening to capitalist financiers, and embark whole-heartedly upon internationalism.

This is my appreciation of the essence in Hobson's opposition to imperialism. While the heretic in him as an economist did not allow him to say it so plainly, the newspaper correspondent in him insisted that he stated his message in sensational manichaean bold strokes of all good and all bad.

Let us now return to the contrast which Hobson established between colonialism and imperialism. Colonialism, against which imperialism was contrasted for definitional purposes, was considered good, because in its best sense it was "*a natural* overflow of nationality; its test [was] the power of colonists to transplant the civilization they represent to the new, natural, social environment in which they find themselves."[23] This test has three parts, none of which imperialism could pass, some of which spurious colonialism could pass, but all of which colonialism, by virtue of definition, could pass easily. The three parts of the test deal with problems of imperialism, as seen by Hobson from the strictly hegemonic and European points of view. The problems deal with the *difficulties* of imperialism for Europeans, the *dangers* of *imperialism* to the European civilization, and the *costliness* of imperialism for the hegemonic and the other competing European powers.

Imperialism, compared to colonialism, was *difficult* for the following reasons: (1) the compulsion involved in government, the absence of true self-government; (2) the unassimilable nature and the preponderance of the natives; and (3) the inhospitable nature of those territories for

European habitation. Imperialism was considered *dangerous* because of these outcomes: (1) it led to the development of separate nationalisms in Europe[24] which served as the bases for animosities among competing European empires;[25] and (2) it interfered with the liberties and the existence of the "weaker" or "lower" races, and Hobson feared that such interference through contact with the white civilization would "stimulate in them a corresponding excess of national self-consciousness."[26] Imperialism was considered *costly* for the following reasons: (1) trade with the imperialized areas was not as profitable as it was believed; in fact, Hobson believed that trade with these areas was not needed; and (2) the costs of the numerous wars fought in the imperialist quests were not worth the gains in trade.

Hobson believed that war could be avoided altogether, if some institutionalized and concerted European exploitation of these lands was adopted. This would, of course, not only bring about peace amongst Europeans, it would also maximize the exploitation of these distant and impossible lands.

For our purposes, Hobson's entire thesis that imperialism was bad for Europe stands or falls on the validity which he attached to the distinction he made between colonialism and imperialism. The conceptual problem, then, is the extent to which the "bad-good" distinction which translates into "difficult-easy," "dangerous-safe," "costly-not costly," and, therefore, "useless-useful" contrasts, could be considered factually true, analytically sound, and, therefore, historically proper.

If Hobson's thesis hinges on the solidness of these contrasts, then the guiding question is this: Are these differences real enough to let Hobson's contrasting comparison between colonialism and its excessive derivative, imperialism, stand? We do not think so.

Briefly then, on the matter of early European settlements in the Americas, the Caribbean Islands, Australia, and New Zealand, there ought to be no doubt that these early settlements were not easy. The climates must have appeared different, even perhaps oppressive, the vegetation strange in parts, and the natives, whether few and peaceful or not, must have been the most harassing. But these early settlements became successful because the settlers were able to adapt to the conditions of their new homes. They *had* to adapt because they *had* to accumulate capital. Among other things, they found some parts of these lands suitable for agriculture as their civilization knew it.

At the time, they found these lands sparsely populated, by their standards; and they were able to control the native population by, among other things, systematic genocide. All these factors conspired to make the early settlements appear to Hobson to have been relatively easier compared to the later attempts at establishing settlements in Africa and Asia. These early settlements must have been gradual at first, but the important thing to note is that they were steady. As the Europeans learnt more and more about the "new" areas, more and more of them came, and the frontiers moved forward.

There was the *need* for the early settlers to move to their new homes. What Hobson was therefore suaging against in his arguments was not settlements in the tropical areas *per se*. His arguments revolved around the need for such settlements in the late nineteenth century, and the efficiency of exploitation. His position was that there was no *need* for embarking on the difficult settlements in the tropics, since without such settlements, and the wars they engendered, the same, if not higher, gains could be obtained.

Hobson should have known, however, that had there been the need, for example, had Europe been so over-populated as to necessitate the exportation of surplus Europeans to no other part of the world but to the tropical and sub-tropical lands, this would have been done without the slightest hesitation. Nothing would have stopped the British, for example, from using the lands of the "lower" races as a "dumping ground for surplus population, including criminals, paupers and never-do-wells."[27] The adverse tropical conditions and the cost it would have entailed (in terms of European lives) for any extended European settlements would not have appeared enough to deter the ideology of capital accumulation from rationalizing and accepting such settlements as right, had the need been apparent.[28]

In fact, where such needs had appeared necessary for the purpose of establishing footholds in Africa and Asia for the unequal trade of the late nineteenth century, the European presence, admittedly not in large numbers and not over extended periods, was not absent. Any study will confirm that more and more Europeans had been in the tropical and the sub-tropical areas as they were needed there to prepare the grounds for the pursuit of capital accumulation since the late fifteenth century. In other words, Europeans had been in the tropical and sub-tropical parts of the world, to the extent that their purposes dictated, long before Hobson felt the compulsion to dramatize such presence as impossible for climatic and other reasons.

The point is that the same arguments which Hobson advanced in support of his view could have been used against the permanent settlements of European population in those parts of the world where the pressures of nascent capitalism drove them earlier for permanent habitation. An important question is this: Suppose Hobson's internationalist recommendation for the joint-European nations' exploitation of the African and Asian peoples and their resources had been institutionalized, *how* would this European institution have exploited these parts of the world? Would the institution not have needed Europeans in these parts for the exploitation? Or would the mere institution of this internationalism have banished the inhabitability of these areas for Europeans? This and the other questions can be answered only within the strict context of the historic specificity of the capitalist world-system.

With respect to the profitability of trade with the areas of over-extended colonialism, Hobson was a little hasty in calling such trade unprofitable. The period 1870–1900 was too short for any such conclusion. Assuming trade was really unprofitable, the capitalist rationality does not exclude the type of investment that imperialism was making in the peoples, lands, and other resources of the "lower" races. Time was needed to "case the joint," as it were, and to prepare the natives to need European products and to generally co-operate with the exploiters in exploiting the areas.[29] Hobson's own statistics show that in India, where enough time had been allowed for the imperialist quest to prove itself, trade was not that unprofitable.[30] Without necessarily saying that all the lands of the "lower" races were worth the imperialist efforts in the very short run, it is in order to say that Hobson should not have judged profitability only by immediate trade statistics.

There were other gains, as he knew. There were jobs for the "boys," and there were, and had been, lots to look for in the form of preciosities. The capitalists simply had more confidence in the ability of the natives to work, and in their ability to make them work, than Hobson had. No capitalists — individuals or nations — worth their capital would fail to invest in resources, and would fail to allow *ample time* to indicate whether the investments are worth it or not. In Hobson's context, 30 years is definitely too short a time for the bold conclusion he drew from his trade, investment, and war-costs statistics.[31]

Indeed, for capitalists, when is trade too small or unprofitable to justify or warrant its termination? And since when did a capitalist abandon activity in any market, which only *appeared* unprofitable, when there was the prospect of increase in the profits in that market over a reasonable time? Hobson's argument should have been based not on the smallness of trade, and minor fluctuations in it, but on the potential for higher levels of trade and high rates of return. These are the time-honoured measures of worthy capitalist investment.[32]

The main argument of Hobson in this regard was that trade was unprofitable for the nations, but highly profitable for the few capitalist financiers. If Hobson had approached the argument in terms of the primacy of capital accumulation in Europe, in the hands of a few financiers, and away from the rest of the world, he would have realized that the situation could not have been otherwise, certainly not in the circumstances of 1900. This concentration of capital is what capitalism is all about.

The third argument of Hobson's case against facile colonialism is the unassimilability of the peoples of the over-extended areas. On this point, it is consonant with Hobsonian preference for true colonialism over imperialism to infer that, if the people of these parts of the world could have been wiped out like the aborigines of his true colonial areas, and if the climate had been the least bit hospitable for European habitation, then the best thing that could have been done, since exploitation and colonialism were inevitable, would have been to kill the natives off to make it impossible for perverse nationalism to develop. This would have removed the principal imperialist problem as Hobson saw it. The problem existed precisely because the peoples of the "lower" races persisted in large numbers. And the danger, as Hobson saw it, was that their contact with European values could let loose from them a "perverse" form of national consciousness, which could be detrimental to the entire European civilization.

On this latter point, Hobson did not read properly what was going on, and had been going on, in parts of Asia and Africa. The persistence and the resistance of the people of these areas might have interfered with smooth and efficient exploitation, but these were overcome to an appreciable extent by the co-option of the ruling classes, and subsequently, of the peoples themselves into European ways. True, nationalisms of sorts reared their heads in these parts, some 50 years after Hobson wrote, but that is not the point. The point is that, even when this did happen, it posed very little threat to the European civilization and its exploitation of the world. This is because the presumed unprofitability of trade with these areas, and the exaggerated inhospitability of their lands, did not prevent the subordinate integration of their economies and societies into the world capitalist system.

It was precisely because this integration had removed any venom which the rebellious nationalisms could have had that *the idioms of these nationalisms were European.* So European were these idioms[33] that when the nationalisms did raise their heads they proved not to be ugly heads threatening European civilization but petty little heads demanding to be parts, even *imitative, subordinate,* and *dependent* parts of the European civilization.

Finally, how could the internationalism which Hobson so much wanted to see institutionalized have stopped the occurrence of such perverse nationalism? Europeans had no choice but to have contact and increasingly so with the so-called lower races.

Since we conceive of imperialism not merely as a war-causing phenomenon but as a phenomenon centred on world-wide exploitation for the purpose of capital accumulation, we have based our discussion of Hobson's arguments on the distinction he sought to establish between real colonialism and real imperialism. Our argument has been that the differences he mentioned are false, at best weak. We have endeavoured to show that the "inhabitability" argument was lame, that the "unprofitability" argument was too hasty, and that the "perverse nationalism" argument, which hinged on the "unassimilability" factor, was exaggerated.

The Eurocentric difference he establishes between "genuine nationalism," which leads to real colonialism, and "perverse nationalism," which he claims leads to imperialism, or facile colonialism, cannot but blind Hobson to the continuity of imperialism thesis. His restricted concern with the turn of the nineteenth century period could not have enlightened him on earlier experiences and their similarities with those of his period. Such enlightenment would have reduced any worth which the differences he postulated may have had, or, perhaps, even obliterated them altogether.

This is so because all the arguments Hobson advanced against "imperialism" and in favour of "colonialism," in his chosen period, could have been advanced against both colonialism and the "colonial areas" of earlier dates. For, indeed, what were Canadian and Australian colonialisms of the nineteenth century, if not imperialism, as Hobson understood it, of earlier capitalist periods. The only worthwhile difference is that, through time and intensive European participation, Canada and Australia had "matured" into respectability to appear falsely as the valued products of genuine nationalisms which had never been perverse in their extra-territorial expressions.

The Incurable Eurocentric Urge

This is our reason for believing that colonialism and imperialism, as Hobson distinguishes between them in the late nineteenth century, are merely different phases of the same phenomenon in its essentials. Taken separately, their forms may differ in appearance; but in their substance and function, with respect to the dominating theme of capitalist evolution, namely the capital accumulation process, they are the same. We warned earlier that the deceptions which so easily attach themselves to historical concepts should be watched carefully. Hobson's is a case where this caveat was not appreciated.

But why did Hobson, an elegant thinker and compassionate believer in social justice, not do historical justice to the concept he treated so brilliantly? The answer is simple. Hobson fell into the ubiquity of the Eurocentric trap of concerning himself with his chosen period alone in treating his subject, without feeling the compulsion to look back, in the context of the proper historical specificity, into the origins of world-history. This led him to ignore any link between his period and relevant earlier periods insofar as this link may relate his concepts to the theme of world-history and its dominant continuities.

Once he fell into this trap, Hobson could not extricate himself. He tightened the grip of this trap on himself even further by appearing to be worried more by the sight and the thought of inter-European wars within his memory. Throughout the discourse, Hobson displayed a clear case of Eurocentric amnesia to the fact that the Americas, for example, in their early imperialist periods, had many inter-European wars fought there, as well as over them in Europe proper.

From the point of view of the continuity of capitalist imperialism thesis, the great mark of the Eurocentric perspective is the subordination of world-history to the history of Europe, or its subordination of world-history to the histories of the hegemonic powers. What is lost in all this is the historical significance of the constancy of the lot of the non-Europeans of the world. To Eurocentrics, the tendency is to view world-history as though it were coterminous with the history of the interests and the doings of a hegemonic power, and not as a history of a system with a dynamism, independent of the identity of a particular hegemonic power. And thus, as dominant powers changed, the world appeared changed also to Eurocentrics. From our perspective, we believe it to be a self-evident fact that once nascent capitalism from Europe emerged to dominate the world, there was no chance that any of the other decadent feudalisms in the world at the time, and since, could produce a world-history hegemonic power for a long time to come. Whichever European nation held hegemony, in world-history terms, would have made very little, a mere footnote, difference to the world, and in the lot of non-Europeans in it, insofar as this history was motivated by accumulation of capital, as it appears in fact to have been.

The Post-Hobson Radicals

Our aim in this section is not to review post-Hobson radicals in all their complexity,[34] but to show that, no matter how much they may or may not differ, they continue the radical tradition, initiated by Hobson, of tampering with the world-system continuity of capitalist imperialism by being over-precise in their periodization of the phenomenon and by being Eurocentric in their ontology of it. We cannot proceed, however, without making the observation that post-Hobson radicals cannot be identified without reference to their preoccupation with the similarities and differences between Hobson's and Lenin's views on imperialism. Since it became clear, just before the First World War, that the works of Marx could suggest that capitalism need not be expansive, it has become difficult to distinguish the radical from the rightist Marxist in their views on imperialism.[35]

Thus, apart from the clear case of the liberals, there are very few writers who cannot be regarded, in one sense or the other, as radicals. The post-Hobson radical camp is so crowded with such fine shades of opinion that it becomes a difficult and risky business to group writers within this camp.[36] For this reason, it will be foolhardy of us to attempt to discuss, in the deserving detail, the spectrum of views held by the many writers who are regarded, or who regard themselves, as post-Hobson radicals.

Suffice it to say that post-Hobson radicals, by and large, maintain Hobson's revulsion for war, his conception of imperialism as a political choice of policy arising out of the capitalist economic taproot, his hatred for capitalist financiers, and his focus on the activities of hegemonic power. They maintain all these things with a clear concern for contemporaneity. They continue the Hobsonian penchant for illustrating the changes in the arithmetics of imperialism with dubious statistics. Some of them are even reluctant to use the term "capitalist imperialism"; they prefer "economic imperialism."[37]

Just as the Boer War produced Hobson's *imperialism*, every major war since has produced a new crop of radical writings on the subject.[38]

What is significant about radical writings on imperialism is not that they have not been able to disengage the study of imperialism from that of war. They continue to see imperialism as a phenomenon which either caused a particular war, or as a phenomenon which must of necessity take on a new form after wars. What is significant is that post-Hobson radicals have not been able to resist the compulsion to take it for granted that imperialism is a nineteenth-century phenomenon of sorts.

The vocation of a large number of these radicals is to revise and up-date Hobson's formulation through criticizing Lenin's in order to make the conceptions of these two writers appear compatible, so that they can have a distinctly post-Hobson formulation, a Hobson-Lenin basis, for the purpose of identifying contemporary imperialism in terms of hegemonic activities.[39]

A speciality within this vocation is debating the tenets of the Hobson-Lenin model of imperialism. It consists of debating the extent to which it could be said that Lenin owed something to Hobson. The vocation consists of showing that the two writers, as different as they may appear, were writing in mutually supporting roles.[40] The pros and cons in this debate should not concern us here, because it is of little use to us in this work; but it is worth mentioning that we do not find this particular debate enlightening in that it is obvious to us that the two conceptions of imperialism as a late nineteenth-century European phenomenon must be mutually supportive, if in nothing at all, in their Eurocentric and over-precise conceptions of the phenomenon.

The real purpose behind this vocation is to show that the imperialist phenomenon has been undergoing changes that are clearly discernible at intervals. And as these radicals pronounce the phenomenon changed, the question becomes whether, in the light of what gave rise to their imperialism initially in the 1870s, and in light of what has happened since in "Europe" and in the world, it could be said that capitalism can exist without imperialism.[41] This question means nothing more than whether state expansionist policies of industrial capitalism can and, therefore, ought to be limited, if not eliminated. This is precisely what we described at the beginning of this chapter as the legacy that Hobson had left later radicals, and around which their differences revolve.

Those among the radicals who believe that capitalism needs imperialism to survive, if not to thrive, see their reasons for this view in the changing forms and rationales of world capitalism as conducted by the United States. And those who believe otherwise explain their positions in terms which detract in no way from Hobson's initial statement.[42]

We do not think that the question above on which radicals since Hobson have spent so much thought is "*the* question of imperialism." In fact, we do not think that this question is a question at all. Certainly, we do not think it is a theoretical question, in the good sense of the word *theory*. There is no way in which the question can be answered satisfactorily within the theoretical necessities of capitalism. The answers to this question along the lines of overproduction/underproduction, rising organic composition of capital, surplus or super profit, capital export, and the bribing of the worker aristocracy, monopolies and transnationals, etc.,[43] have all proved inadequate. Neither of these elements of the assumed necessities of capital can account for imperialism over its entire course of history. We would never know whether capitalism could ever have done, or can ever do, without imperialism. Capitalism was never put to the test of doing without imperialism, nor is it likely to be put to such a test in the near future.

On this same question, "Does capitalism have to be imperialistic?" Lynn Richards says this:

> Although this question is important — and I believe, answerable in the affirmative — I would suggest that until such time as a "way out" is discovered, the confluence of a logical causal relationship and impressive evidence as to the existence of such a relationship is scientifically adequate. If the logic is good enough, all such proposed "ways out" will always be destroyed by the question, "Why has this not been done?"[44]

86

Indeed, why has this not been done?

Thomas Weisskopf undertook, in a critical evaluation of theories of imperialism, to decide whether it is "national interest" or "class interest" that is responsible for American imperialism. This exercise is a waste of time and doomed to failure, in view of the close relationship between the two interests; and Weisskopf's essay proves it as such. Robert Wolfe, after pronouncing Lenin's thesis of imperialism as "open to criticism on several grounds,"[45] declares that "there is no inherent economic *necessity* for certain aspects of American imperialism."[46] This view is to be found in the same collection of essays where James O'Connor's "The Meaning of Economic Imperialism" believes Lenin's view of the subject is "not very useful today."[47]

Theorizing on imperialism will remain on a low and embarrassing level in radical circles for as long as they continue to do what Hobson did, namely take the short duration of activities of hegemonic powers as the totality of the phenomenon, and for as long as they refuse to follow what the works of the best among them indicate, namely that capitalism has been imperialist from its very beginning.[48] It has to be, because it began as a world-system centred in Europe, when Europe chanced upon the opportunity to use the rest of the world to resolve its feudal crisis. "Europe" has continued to do so because it has known no other way for 500 years, and, in any case, any other credible way appears too expensive for "Europe" to contemplate, as it would entail the probable loss of European dominance in the world-economy.

We consider it enough to do as Frank does, that is, to consider "history as theory." This is all that is needed to escape the Eurocentric tampering with the continuity of imperialism thesis, just enough to realize that capitalism is imperialist.

Notes

1. J.A. Hobson, *Imperialism: A Study* (Allen and Unwin, London, 1951), p. 3.
2. Hobson (see note 1 above), p. 243.
3. Hobson (see note 1 above), p. 3.
4. G. Arrighi, *The Geometry of Imperialism: The Limits of Hobson's Paradigm* (NLB, London, 1978), p. 33.
5. Arrighi (see note 4 above), p. 112.
6. Hobson (see note 1 above), p. 6.
7. Hobson (see note 1 above), p. 6.
8. Hobson (see note 1 above), p. 6.

9. Hobson (see note 1 above), pp. 6–7.
10. Hobson (see note 1 above), p. 8.
11. Hobson (see note 1 above), p. 8.
12. Hobson (see note 1 above), p. 10.
13. Hobson (see note 1 above), p. 8.
14. Hobson (see note 1 above), p. 11.
15. Hobson (see note 1 above), p. 11.
16. See my *A World-System Critique of Eurocentric Conceptions of Capitalism* (Mimeo, 1980).
17. Our argument here is not based on any blind case of vulgar Marxism that fails to acknowledge the influence of the superstructure and its importance in determining/defining the historical forms. Our position is that superstructural explanation without reference to the particular fundamentals of economic forms could be misleading.
18. Arrighi (see note 4 above), p. 33.
19. This is interesting. Hobson does not realize the truth of the matter that hierarchical social systems must have varying degrees of assimilation with respect to the core of the culture. When all become equally assimilable, we will be approaching an egalitarian system and a homogeneous culture.
20. It takes no more than the most common of commonsense to realize that such preponderance must have existed in most of the areas where the white man first ventured outside Europe.
21. Hobson (see note 1 above), pp. 252–253.
22. The first part of Hobson's book deals with the economic aspect of the answers to this question and the second part is devoted to the political and other superstructural aspects. However, the book is to be read as a whole to appreciate the subtlety and the Eurocentric elegance of Hobson's overall argument.
23. Hobson (see note 1 above), p. 7.
24. Hobson (see note 1 above), p. 7.
25. Hobson (see note 1 above), p. 11.
26. Hobson (see note 1 above), p. 11.
27. Hobson (see note 1 above), p. 118.
28. The advice, "Go West young man, go West," would have been offered in its equivalent form as "Go to the tropics young man, go to the tropics."
29. Hobson himself formulated the case supporting this view very well on pp. 71–73 of his book (see note 1 above). His argument against the case is very weak.
30. India is a case in point. Here the statistics Hobson provides to discredit imperialist trade are not very convincing. See chapter 2, especially pp. 35–37 of his book (note 1 above).
31. Eric Williams, in his *Capitalism and Slavery* (University of North Carolina Press, Chapel Hill, N.C., 1944), p. 52, tells us that "it was the negro slaves who made these sugar colonies (of the West Indies) the most precious colonies ever recorded in the annals of imperialism," and on p. 54 he refers to "the amazing value of these West Indian islands with individual mainlands (North American) colonies." He states further on p. 209 that "it was only with the loss of the American colonies in 1783 that Britain turned to the serious exploitation of her Indian possession." This means the Indian possession had some use for Britain in the past, if it could be used to cushion the impact of the great shock the British economy must have received upon losing the American colonies. Can we ignore all this in assessing the economic value of imperialism by reference only to a restricted 30-year period?
32. If it would not have been unfair to Hobson's argument, one could have pointed to the persistence of the so-called "lower" races as an indication of the weakness of his argument. It is strange that Hobson seems to have lacked the

characteristic of massive confidence that men of his period seemed to have had in the progressive role of technology. Hobson wrote a book, *The Evolution of Modern Capitalism: A Study of Machine Production*, of which Siegelman says, "Hobson was dealing here with the social consequences of capital formation — an area which he regarded throughout his life as central to the large problem of establishing a just and human social order" (Siegelman, introduction to Hobson, *Imperialism: A Study* [n.p., London, 1905], p. xi). This quote creates the misconception that capital formation began with industrial or machine production.

33. The idioms included Western European liberal and Marxist terms such as: equality, fairness, independence, political parties, proletariat, workers, capitalism, full employment, higher wages, investment profit, etc.

34. This section is very interesting for many reasons, but it has been presented in a narrative manner because, after the lengthy discussion of Hobson's work, we think the arguments ought to be clear. The interested reader may refer to some of the references below.

35. For excellent reading on this, see the chapter on "Development of the Theories of Capitalist Imperialism: The Neo-Marxists," in E.M. Winslow, *The Pattern of Imperialism: A Study in Theories of Power* (Octagon Press, New York, 1972), pp. 149–188.

36. To illustrate the risk involved: using imperialism as a policy and not a "necessity" of capitalism as the measure for radicals, we could include in this camp names such as Kautsky, Hilferding, Bauer, Parker T. Moon, Arghiri Emmanuel, and Al Szymanski. And when we use as the measure the concern with monopolies and their incarnation, the MNCs, we could include Hymer, Magdoff, Baran, and Sweezy. The risk lies in being unfair to some outstanding scholars who have written extensively on the subject, and for this reason, it defies any easy categorization. Just because Samir Amin, for example, believes that with a proper understanding of the active "role of money and credit in accumulation" it is possible for capitalism to operate in a society with only the bourgeois-proletariat confrontation is no reason why the world-system thrust of his other works should be ignored. See Samir Amin, *Imperialism and Unequal Exchange* (Monthly Review Press, New York, 1977), pp. 104–105, and other references below. Similarly, the works by Baran and Sweezy on MNC and militarism should not detract from their other works with world-system significance. See Paul Baran and Paul Sweezy, *Monopoly Capital* (Monthly Review Press, New York, 1966); "Notes on the Theory of Imperialism," in K.T. Fann and D.C. Hodges, eds., *Readings in U.S. Imperialism* (Porter Sargent, Boston, 1971), pp. 69–84.

37. See Winslow (note 35 above), pp. 92–93 for the difference. See also James O'Connor, "The Meaning of Economic Imperialism," in K.T. Fann and D.C. Hodges (note 36 above), pp. 23–67.

38. The Viet Nam war in particular appears to have produced many radicals on imperialism in the United States, or at least brought radical writers into prominence. Currently their writings can be found in the *Review of Radical Political Economics*, a publication of the Union of Radical Political Economists, and in the *Insurgent Sociologist*, see the special issue on "Imperialism and the State," 7, no. 2 (Spring 1977).

39. Harry Magdoff, *The Age of Imperialism* (Monthly Review Press, New York, 1969) and Michael Hudson, *Super Imperialism: The Economic Strategy of American Empire* (Holt, Rinehart and Winston, New York, 1972) are good examples of the contemporary emphasis on imperialism. See Al Szymanski, "Capital Accumulation on a World Scale and the Necessity of Imperialism," *Insurgent Sociologist* 8, no. 2 (1977): 35–53, and Magdoff's response in pp. 106–112. In addition, see their exchange in *Monthly Review*, May 1978: 48–61.

40. Because Hobson's work is so clear to read, the vitriolic exchanges centre mainly on Lenin's work — what he wrote and what he meant. See note 39 above for good examples.

41. In addition to the references above on Baran and Sweezy, Magdoff, and Szymanski, see O'Connor (note 36 above), and Robert Wolfe, "American Imperialism and the Peace Movements," in Fann and Hodges (note 36 above). See also Thomas Weisskopf, "Theories of American Imperialism: A Critical Evaluation," *The Review of Radical Political Economics* 6, no. 3 (Fall 1974): 41–60; Lynn Richards, "The Context of Foreign Aid, Modern Imperialism," *The Review of Radical Political Economics* 4, no. 1 (Winter 1972), especially pp. 53–58; and other essays in Fann and Hodges (see note 36 above), and in Steven J. Rosen and James R. Kurth, eds., *Testing Theories of Economic Imperialism* (D.C. Heath, Lexington, Mass., 1974).

42. Compare Thomas Weisskopf's essay with Lynn Richards'.

43. Arghiri Emmanuel has added a new factor, what he calls the social factor of "white-settlers." See his "White-Settler Colonialism and the Myth of Investment Imperialism," *New Left Review* 73 (May–June 1973): 35–57.

44. Lynn Richards (see note 41 above), p. 53.

45. Wolfe (see note 41 above), p. 313.

46. Wolfe (see note 41 above), p. 322.

47. Fann and Hodges (see note 36 above), p. 44.

48. US radicals are always referring to works by Baran, Sweezy, Amin, Frank, and others and yet they always always miss the continuity of imperialism thesis implicit in those works. See the *Insurgent Sociologist* 7, no. 2 (1977), for example.

Chapter Five

The Marxist Conception of Imperialism

The Legacy of Marx in Lenin's Theory of Imperialism

One cannot discuss the Marxist conception of imperialism without beginning with Lenin's theory of imperialism. It is in order, however, to start with a discussion of the legacy that Marx (and Engels) bequeathed the Leninist conception of imperialism, for the simple reason that, after all and with good reason, this intellectual tradition bears Marx's name.

It is incontestable that Marx and Engels dismissed some of the early events in the process of the development of capitalism without due regard for the implications of these events for world-history. This is not in itself strange. In fact, it is understandable, since, as it is universally known, the vocation of Marx and Engels covered principally the "maturation" and the "terminalities" of capitalism, as they reasoned them at their time.

If Marx and Engels consigned what we would regard as some of the significant events of the capitalist world-system to the unimpressive heap of "prehistory" of capital, it was because they believed so much in the progressive mission of capital, which they considered in the national contexts to the exclusion of the world-system context.

It would be unfair to accuse Marx and Engels of being Eurocentric in their conception of imperialism, because Marx stressed time and again that "it should not be forgotten that the horizon of his work on the discussion of historical development [was] essentially European,"[1] and that "in *Capital* he had studied only the genesis of capitalism in Western Europe."[2] It is, therefore, not surprising when Winslow tells us that "we shall look in vain in the writings of Karl Marx for a theory of modern imperialism as such,"[3] and further that in one place Marx used the term "imperialism," but he had in mind merely a political system called empire, supported by bourgeois elements for the purpose of exploiting labour.[4]

At times Marx made it appear that capitalism, if it chose, could be non-expansive; and at other times he made it appear that capitalism had no choice in the matter; it has to be expansive.[5] Despite this equivocation, the core of the matter is precisely as Winslow puts it:

> Marx is the father of the idea that capitalism is responsible in modern times for the creation of surplus products for which it must find ever-expanding markets or die, and in seeking them fight to the death. It makes little difference whether he called this out-thrust of national capitalist systems "imperialism" or not. "Capitalism" was an all embracing term to Marx and he had no need for any other.[6]

We shall note two very crucial points at this juncture. The first is that the Marxist theory of imperialism cannot be separated from the Marxist theory of capitalist development without some damage being done to the theory of imperialism. The Marxist conception of imperialism is to be considered essentially, therefore, as part of the Marxist conception of the development of capitalism in Western Europe. The second is that, from the very beginning, the ontological referents of the concept are cast concretely in terms of "modern surpluses" — modern surplus products, which later become modern surplus capital in its centralized and concentrated form, and modern expanding markets. The problem with the Marxist conception of imperialism is precisely its inability to break away from the *over-precise* clamps of *modern surpluses*, seen through the ethno-centric spectacles of a late-nineteenth-century modern Europe.

As much as it is true that the Marxist conception of imperialism is intrinsically linked with its theory of capitalist development, we agree with Palma that we can still refer to imperialism in Lenin's sense as a theory. This is because, as he says, "It is absolutely legitimate to use the concept of imperialism to designate only that aspect of capitalist development which has related the fortunes of the advanced and the backward areas within the world capitalist system, and to even speak of a theory of imperialism [provided we take pains to distinguish between the wider and the restricted aspects of the theory]."[7] Our present concern is not the theory of capitalist development but that of imperialism in Lenin's sense, and to the extent that the two theories are separable, we shall try to separate them. In fact, in order to establish an organic relationship between the two, we need to "separate" them first.

The legacy which Marx left us to understand imperialism is admittedly flimsy, because it is equivocal and it admits Eurocentricity. Yet we do not believe this is a good excuse for the various Eurocentric Marxist views of the subject. What has become the Marxist "orthodoxy" on the subject of imperialism hinges on Marx's idea that imperialism is inherent in capitalism, that is, that capitalism must *expand* or die. The problem with this orthodoxy is that capitalism is left no other alternative. The orthodox Marxist conception of the subject is based on the views of Luxemburg and Lenin, which essentially reiterated Marx's position that capitalism had to expand. Luxemburg and Lenin, in their different ways, defended this view against other Marxists, like Hilferding, Bauer, Kautsky, and Bukharin, who held the equally Marxist view that capitalism need not expand in order not to die.[8]

Barratt Brown has provided a succinct description of the Marxist model. He writes, "The essence of the marxist model is that capitalism contains by its very nature an expansionist force — the production of capital to produce more capital. As distinct from [other and earlier economic forms], those based on the ownership of *industrial* capital must expand or die." (Emphasis added.)[9] If the question is: Why must industrial capitalism expand or die? the answer is that it is because of the Marxist belief that, with increasing industrialization, the organic composition of capital would tend to rise with the consequence of a falling rate of profit. This will occur unless corrective measures are taken to prevent it. But the capitalist system ceases to be such, when capitalists indulge in fundamental corrective actions.[10] So long as the system remains capitalist, it must experience this tendency. The only way the system could cope with this tendency would be to expand to incorporate areas that are not fully incorporated in the system. Since this is the case, some Marxists believe that imperialism, their monopoly stage of capitalism, the expansionary imperative of capitalism at a certain stage, is an essential and inherent part of the capitalist mode of production.

An allied, even if muted, theme in the Marxist explanation of imperialism is the *underconsumptionist* hypothesis, which holds that highly developed capitalist economies tend to produce more than could be consumed, simply because the workers in these economies, who buy the largest part of the products, are not paid enough by their capitalist employers to purchase all that is produced. At the moment, whether the twin Marxist belief in the rising organic composition of capital and the underconsumption hypothesis is true or not should not detain us.

For the present, we shall refer only to Lenin's conception of imperialism in order to show that the orthodox Marxist view of imperialism, while different from the liberal and the radical views, is no less Eurocentric. Like Hobson, Lenin approached the definition of imperialism with some caution; but in Lenin's case, it was not until chapter seven of his *Imperialism: The Highest Stage of Capitalism* that he assembled all the essential elements which together defined imperialism as "a definite and very high stage of [capitalist] development,"[11] and then, in "the briefest possible" form, as the "monopoly stage of capitalism."[12]

On account of the many disagreements on the exact meaning of Lenin's conception of imperialism, it is necessary to present his definition at some length. In his own words,

> Imperialism emerged as the development and direct continuation of the fundamental attributes of capitalism in general. But capitalism only became capitalist imperialism at a definite and very high stage of its development, when certain of its fundamental attributes began to be transformed into their opposites, when the features of a period of transition from capitalism to a higher social and economic system began to take shape and reveal themselves all along the line. Economically the main thing in this process is the substitution of capitalist monopolies for capitalist free competition. Free competition is the fundamental attribute of capitalism, and of commodity production generally. Monopoly is the exact opposite of free competition;....

> If it were necessary to give the briefest possible definition of imperialism we should have to say that imperialism is the monopoly stage of capitalism. Such definition would include what is most important for, on the one hand, finance capital is the bank capital of a few big monopolist banks, merged with the capital of the monopolist combined manufacturers; and, on the other hand, the division of the world in the transition from [the free for all] colonial policy, to a colonial policy of monopolistic possession of the territory of the world which has been completely divided up.[13]

Because brief definitions are always inadequate, Lenin provides us with a listing of the five *essential* features of imperialism. They are: (1) the concentration of production and capital *creating monopolies*; (2) the merger between the bank and industrial capitals into *creating finance capital*; (3) the *export of capital becoming* more important than the export of commodities; (4) international *monopolies sharing* the world among themselves; and, as a result, (5) *monopolies completing* the division of the world among the greater capitalist powers.[14] These five essential features are processes which are supposed to have started precisely at the industrial phase of capitalism. Herein lie the origins of the Marxist over-precise conception of imperialism, its Eurocentric property.

Marxists demarcate three periods in the history of capitalism. According to Amin, a versatile Marxist, they distinguish between: (1) the period when capitalism was being formed — the "prehistory" that ends with the beginning of the Industrial Revolution of the eighteenth and nineteenth centuries; (2) the period of the flowering of the capitalist mode of production at the centre, marked by the Industrial Revolution; and (3) the imperialist monopoly period beginning at the end of the nineteenth century.[15] It is clear from the description of the third period that, to many Marxists, imperialism is not just a word to be understood closer to its etymological origins, but, as Kemp explains, in "a technical sense which has to be carefully distinguished from the variable meaning attached to it by historians and others."[16] The technical meaning resides in the peculiarities of the "monopoly stage" of the development of capitalism. Lenin's contribution to the Marxist theory of imperialism is that he identified the *modus operandi* of the third period of capitalist development, and its implications for the world-economy, from the point of view of European dominance in the world-economy, as imperialist.

To reiterate, what is missing is a view of the world-economy on its own terms as an evolving system, European dominance notwithstanding.

In this regard, our point of contention, in fact our worry is that we find it strange that the users of Marx's methodology and the followers of his philosophy, who pride themselves on Marxism's sensitivity to the flow of human social history in both its objective and subjective subtleties, should hang so tenaciously onto the admitted Eurocentric biases in Marx's theory of capitalist development. Our immediate concern being the Marxist theory of imperialism, and not the Marxist theory of capitalist development as such,[17] what we find particularly strange is that the Leninist line on the subject should be allowed to mar the minimally acceptable definition of imperialism, as the world-system implications of the "externalization" or the "internationalization" of the capital accumulation enterprise, in all its phases and stages, by the obscurantist insistence that imperialism is at once the "monopoly" and the "highest" stage of capitalism.

For our part, the root problem with the Marxist theory of imperialism is that world events which clearly contributed to the accumulation of capital in Europe, prior to the maturation of this capital in the nineteenth century, are not regarded as related to imperialism. The Leninist orthodoxy on the subject excludes the continuity of world involvement in the accumulation enterprise from its very beginning, in the form of "plunder (of wealth and slaves) and the export of capitalist manufactures to the peripheral countries,"[18] from consideration together with the continuing world involvement through "the export of capital, competition for supplies of raw materials and the growth of monopoly,"[19] in a logico-linear manner. To us, then, the question is: Why should there be this sharp distinction between the so-called "prehistory" of capital and the so-called "history" of mature capital? This question is raised because we worry about the following: whether this sharp distinction does not deprive the process of capital accumulation of its historic wholesomeness; that is, whether this sharp distinction does not tamper with the proper explanation of the secular trends in the history of capital accumulation. Our main worry is whether, by viewing imperialism solely in terms of "mature" capital, Marxists have not come to make too much of capital as an already *accumulated thing*, and in the course have neglected some of the earlier participations, contributions, and events which went into accumulating this *thing* called accumulated capital.

These questions are vitally pertinent and cannot be brushed aside by any theory of imperialism which claims to be part of a theory of capitalist development, understood as *"essentially a process of capital accumulation which produces as it evolves modifications in the composition of the productive forces, in resource allocation, in class relations, and in the character of the state; that is, which produces as it evolves modifications in the different structures of society."*[20] The world-system is also a society. And it is not possible to deny that, as the process of capital accumulation evolves, it produces modifications in the structures of the world-system, as a society.

This noted, and recalling our thesis, we intend to suggest that the Marxist conception of imperialism slights the continuity of the capitalist imperialist experience, in terms of the role that the "evolving world" played in the evolving process of capital accumulation in its earlier phases. Our argument is that the Marxist conception freezes the appreciation of the capitalist imperialist phenomenon around certain variables which have meaning and make possible qualitative differences only in terms of Europe's interests and her dominance in this enterprise.

By doing this, the Marxist conception becomes *over-precise* and therefore Eurocentric, just as the radical conception is.

Again recalling our earlier position that we do not think the question is whether or not capitalism is expansive, since it has been expansive all through its history, we intend merely to underline here that the Eurocentric Leninist orthodoxy derives from the basically erroneous belief of Marxists (even if totally acceptable as a convenient Eurocentric methodological device) that the rest of the world is merely an underdeveloped Europe, waiting to be developed by "European capital."

If Lenin's mistake was to attempt to universalize this legacy of Marx to explain world-historical events since the maturation of capital, his problem, as it is widely recognized, lay in trying to understand and explain concrete situations both in developed and underdeveloped capitalist Europe.[21] It was when these and other concrete situations posed problems for Europe that Lenin's study of them evolved into the Marxist theory of imperialism.

Lenin's problem, to say the least, was very difficult. So that even if one accepts the Eurocentric nature of his theory of imperialism as excusable, what is difficult to accept is why post-Lenin Marxists still insist on using this clearly Eurocentric view of capitalist development for the study of the capitalist world-system, the problems of which, because of Europe, are different from Europe's.

As we have seen above, Lenin's conception of imperialism consists of two parts. He first described the phenomenon as the "highest stage," the "last stage," and as a "very high stage" of capitalism; and this was followed by the description of it as the "monopoly stage capitalism." We now proceed to examine these two descriptions in some detail.

The Leninist Orthodoxy: The Fallacy of "the Highest Stage"

With respect to the "highest stage" thesis, we believe that Marxists and other Eurocentrics have made too much of this characteristic revolutionary outburst of Lenin's, in which he imagined the ensemble he detected as peculiar to imperialism to constitute the death knell of capitalism, the final contradiction where attributes begin to transform into their opposites. In fact, hindsight alone would suggest that the thesis is best regarded as simply part of an unfulfilled prophecy or, more correctly, as a wishful expectation, the kind which is not exactly unknown among Marxists. But we cannot dismiss this view of imperialism so lightly because there appears to be too much Eurocentric *method* to this apparently mad thesis.

Keeping in mind the nature of Lenin's problematic vocation, and in particular the sensitivity which characterized his writings (and which tended to breed extreme optimism as well as — some will even say rather than — extreme caution),[22] we prefer to understand the thesis to mean that capitalism, being one of the evolutionary stages of society in history, has to give way to something higher. This ought to happen by virtue of capitalism's very nature as only an intermediate "stage." Whatever Lenin thought imperialism to be, he meant it as an ensemble of historical facts which constituted extreme contradictions for capitalism.

The contradictions were supposed to express the highest notes possible in the development of capitalism. In no sense does this mean that capitalism could not change its form or substance prior to its collapse. It implies, however, by virtue of the word "highest," that before its demise, all succeeding notes in the development of capitalism's contradictions would be comparatively minor in their negation significance. This is to be understood to mean that after capital, in its final form, had become extensive world-wide, by mopping up all the uncolonized parts of the world, it could only become more intensive. By becoming intensive, it transfers its contradictions to non-capitalist parts of the world, where in the course of their capitalization, and for some unexplained reason, the apparent arrest in the proletariat revolutionary momentum in Europe during the First World War would be reversed.

The key point, however, is that capitalism, by going imperialist, that is, by violating its fundamental principle of free competition to become financial capital in substance and monopolistic in form, had opened itself up to intensified fatigues and contradictions it could not cope with, try as hard as it might to contain them. In other words, monopolized financial capital, by fleeing to hide, so to speak, in the "virgin but 'distant' parts of the world," had alerted Lenin to its outer limitations. These limitations would be its final undoing, since it fled with its contradictions, not merely intact, but intensified. Thus, we understand Lenin to mean, by the "highest stage of capitalism," or any variation of this phrase, the simple expectation that the negation of the imperialist chain will signal as well as cause the negation of capitalism, as a stage in history.

We all know by now that imperialism as Lenin saw it in the strict terms of the late nineteenth and early twentieth century European capitalist circumstances did not turn out to be a signal for the immediate collapse of capitalism. If the prophecy had come true, the situation would have been different. But because it did not, it is necessary to ask why it did not. We raise this question not so that we can say, as some radicals generally do, that Lenin's expectations at the time are out of date for today; or that monopolies ruined the prophecy by changing their forms, even if they did not change their substance, to become multinational corporations; or do as some writers have done by suggesting new ways of looking at Lenin's theory. And we raise this question not so that we can separate Lenin's intended meaning from its vulgar interpretations, as Magdoff, for one, does when he rails against some interpretations of Lenin's theory of imperialism as a "crude kind of economic interpretation of history."[23]

We raise this question so that we can suggest that the prophecy proved false because it was based on sensitivities which sought to explain the world in terms of Europe. The sensitivities derived from the same incurable Eurocentric urge to consider the capitalist world-system not as something different from Europe, and something of which Europe is only a part, but as merely Europe writ large. The Eurocentric nature of Lenin's conception derives from Marx's admitted Eurocentric concern. But, in this context, the fault is not necessarily Marx's. Lenin, having taken over Marx's Eurocentric perspective of history and being as preoccupied as he was with European matters at the time of writing, could not but be Eurocentric.

The First World War was in full swing when he wrote. And as a Eurocentric, it would have been surprising if he had not seen the war as cause for a variation in what others before him had seen as imperialism. The circumstances of exile, in which Lenin followed the Russian situation of the time, were not the most ideal for him to break away from the long tradition of Eurocentric theorizing, even if that could have been his intention.

Giovanni Arrighi has stated lately with respect to Marxists, and tellingly, too, that instead of critically clarifying Lenin's theory, Marxists have sought refuge in "ever increasing ambiguities and imprecisions of language."[24] We believe that Lenin's conception of imperialism as the "highest stage" of capitalism is beyond any critical clarification for as long as the criticisms which aim at clarifying it are themselves anchored in Eurocentric thought and terminology.

The Leninist Orthodoxy: Exaggerated Respect for Monopolies as Historic Watershed

Lenin saw his highest stage of capitalism as a *transition* from something that was capitalist to something that would not be capitalist. This transition was seen by Lenin in terms of the contradictions surrounding the fundamental attribute of capitalism — free competition. He listed these contradictions in terms we have presented above. Upon closer study, however, the five contradictions resolve into one fundamental structural contradiction, namely the contradiction of *monopolies.*

The *monopolies* Lenin wrote about were created by the concentration of production and capital. Bank and industrial capitals merged into finance capital; but what was a bigger contradiction was that this finance capital was controlled by these same *monopolies.* And because of this control of finance capital by monopolies, there was another contradiction, the contradiction of the export of capital taking precedence over the export of commodities. Finally, these same monopolies shared the "unclaimed" parts of the world among themselves, thus completing the division of the world among the great capitalist powers.

Tom Kemp is right, therefore, when he states, "Lenin's theory of imperialism put the emphasis on the structural changes in capitalism rather than upon the relations between the metropolitan countries and their colonies...."[25] It is precisely because Lenin put so much emphasis on the structural changes which were clearly European in their meaning and significance that we charge that the Marxist theory is Eurocentric. It did not take the non-European and the metropolitan-colony relations much into account. There would have been nothing wrong with Lenin's Eurocentric theory of imperialism had he not presented it as an explanation of the world to the world, and had it not been generally accepted as such.

Orthodox Marxists, self-proclaimed adherents to the Leninist orthodoxy on imperialism, insist that imperialism should be used in the strictly technical sense to describe the expansionary imperative of the monopoly stage of capitalism. Since we believe that capitalism has been expansive all through its history, we take issue with Kemp when, as an orthodox

Marxist, he merely restates the Leninist line, leaving "others to context it if they please."[26] We take issue with Kemp because, if the emergence of monopolies was the key difference in Lenin's transition, that is, if the emergence of monopolies was the main structural change in Europe, then, from the world-system perspective, it is no mean question to ask: In what substantial way did late nineteenth century monopolies differ from earlier forms of monopolies?[27]

There is no doubt that monopolies made a difference to late nineteenth century Europe and the world at the time. In the case of Europe, monopolies might have even made the qualitative difference which appears to have impressed Lenin so much. We do not intend to belittle this difference. But hindsight, and the conceptual honesty in the world-system methodology, compels us to take note that, at the world level of capitalism, the violation of free competition made no more than a quantitative difference insofar as the expansion of capitalism was concerned. According to Lenin, all that the monopolies did to the world outside Europe was that they extended capitalism to incorporate the non-European areas. There is no evidence that without finance capital monopolies, the "division of the world" would not have occurred. Monopolies merely accelerated and completed the historical trend within the historic domination of the world by capitalism. Late nineteenth century monopolies did not cause it.

There is no doubt that monopolies of the period were the main instruments which capital, having concentrated and centralized itself into finance capital, used to intensify and complete its geographic domination of the world. With this point conceded, it is in order to ask whether monopolies, of the kind Lenin was impressed with, did not simply do for their time what earlier forms of monopolies had done for their times in spreading capitalism. Here we refer to such organized forms as the various royal agencies, which had monopolies in the various areas, the trading companies, and the assorted cartels, which preceded finance capital monopolies. These monopolies were the products of "mature" capital as much as their predecessors were the products of the different phases and stages of maturing capital. If we are not to be *over-precise* in our preoccupation with European interests, therefore, and if we are not to conceive of the world as less important than Europe, in that it is merely an underdeveloped Europe, we will find it difficult to exaggerate the emergence of finance capital monopoly into an incomparable historical watershed within the precise historicity of the capitalist world-system's development.

The historical fact of world implication in the accumulation of capital in Europe should not be sacrificed so easily, without a justification or a reason, definitely not without a protest, to the Eurocentric deity of capital as an accumulated thing. We need to know why the monopoly stage of the late nineteenth century was that different from earlier periods insofar as the expansion of capitalism from its "home" base to non-capitalist areas is concerned. The key to this concern seems to lie in the importance Marxists attach to *accumulated capital* in Europe which ignited the insufficient but necessary conditions of the emergence of a potential labour force, general propagation of division of labour, and with them the evolution of the class of merchants into the capitalist blaze of the eighteenth century, which by the late nineteenth century had reproduced so much capital it had to go outside Europe to capitalize the non-capitalist economies of the pre-capitalist societies. Thus, Marxists are clearly more interested in the role that *accumulated* capital played in Europe, and subsequently outside Europe, than in the *process* of its initial *accumulation*, especially in the roles that pre-capitalist non-European areas played in the early phases of this accumulation.

Many Marxists, including Baran, would admit that "far-flung trade, combined with piracy, outright plunder, slave traffic and discovery of gold, led to a rapid formation of vast fortunes in the hands of Western European merchants."[28] Baran reminds us, however, that "the mere accumulation of merchant capital does not *per se* lead to the development of capitalism ... it was the *scope and the speed* of accumulation ... that played itself a major part in corroding the structure of feudal society, in creating the prerequisites for its ultimate demise." (Emphases added.)[29] The non-European world cannot be excluded from the scope and the speed of this accumulation.

The point at issue is whether in the haste to give a convenient Eurocentric technical meaning to the concept imperialism, Marxists have not relegated to small print the immense contributions made by non-European peoples in the history of the process of the accumulation of capital. The key difference here is whether, from the world-system perspective, the emphasis in the reading of world-history is to be placed on the evolution of *capital accumulation* in its world context, or on *accumulated capital*, its habitation in Europe, and its consequence for the world.[30] The place to begin to discuss world-history, and especially the place of non-Europeans in this history, is in the process of capital accumulation in Europe. It is this process which linked non-European histories and European history to create world-history, and it is still this same process which involves all histories in world-history today. The subordination of the periphery to the dominance of the centre is not adequately explained in terms of the sudden surfeit of capital in Europe which then dictated the incorporation of the rest of the world into the capitalist world-economy, through the instrumentality of monopolies.

Samir Amin does see the merit in this position when he holds emphatically that the phenomenon of underdevelopment is thus merely the result of the persistence of a phenomenon in relation to the transformations taking place at the centre. "Primitive accumulation is not something that belongs only to the pre-history of capital, it is something permanent, contemporary."[31] Amin holds this view, because, even as a Marxist, he does not appear to believe in the exaggerated significance of the export of capital to other parts of the world. He, therefore, warns, "Here too we must distinguish between foreign investments in the periphery and those destined for young countries of the 'central' type.... Neither in function nor in dynamic were these investments identical. The export of capital did not replace the export of goods: on the contrary, it stimulated it."[32]

We can very easily concede the importance of the "monopoly stage of capitalism" without necessarily degrading the importance of the "world-wide and interrelated nature of the commerce [of the period preceding the Industrial Revolution], its direct effect upon the development of the Industrial Revolution, and the heritage which it has left even upon the civilization of today."[33] Recognizing the new-world-creation fact of the early mercantile period in world-history should do no harm to the Marxist theory of imperialism. On the contrary, such a longer historical perspective would show us where part of the wealth came from and how it came to be accumulated. Such a recognition will strengthen the materialist interpretation of history. It will show in much clearer terms, as Marx sought to show for Europe, and as Eric Williams has done for the West Indies of the nineteenth century, that indeed "the decisive forces [in history age] are developing economic forces,"[34] and that "the political and the moral ideas of the age are to be examined in the very closest relation to the economic."[35]

The above shows with some clarity, we believe, that the expansionary imperative of capitalism, upon which the Marxist theory of imperialism hinges, has been present from the very inception of this economic form. The Marxist "selection" of the monopoly stage of capitalism as the age of imperialism, imperialism understood to be the exportation of capital to capitalize "virgin" areas, betrays too much respect for capital, as an accumulated thing, and too little respect for the process of accumulating this thing called capital. The theory, as a result, attaches too much importance and significance to the role that monopolies played at a particular stage in the history of capitalism, and too little significance to the roles that earlier forms of monopolies had played in the capital accumulation process.

The Marxist equation of the monopoly stage of capitalism to the age of imperialism comes about mainly because the major concern was with the internal changes that accumulated capital unleashed in European societies. The neglect is the failure to view these European societal changes in longer historical retrospectives; and the reluctance is the refusal to link these changes to the continuity of the experience of non-European areas in accumulation enterprise.

Before this stage of capitalism, the tone had already been set by past practices for the exportation of capital, when it was necessary and possible. From the world-system perspective, the exportation of capital was not that significant in the sense that it failed to fully incorporate the rest of the world — Africa, Asia, and Latin America — into the "mature" capitalist frame. Paradoxically, it is significant, from the world-system perspective, only in the precise sense that it intensified, or gave sharper form to, the structural deformity which the evolution of capitalism had given to the world-economy up to then. This deformity is what Amin captures so well in his conception of the world-economy as constituted by the relations, and the relationships, between, and within, *central capitalist formations and peripheral formations*.[36] The two formations are qualitatively different; and this difference is what makes it possible for capital to accumulate in the central formations and impossible in the peripheral formations.

Our argument here should not be read as meaning that the monopoly stage of capitalism lacks so much lustre that it can be passed over unnoticed in the flow of world-history. No part of world-history is unremarkable in significance, and certainly its monopoly stage is not unremarkable, when it is clear that the broad tones of the contemporary structure of the world-economy still bear the imprints of the particular set of frantic activities in the world which are associated with the monopoly stage of capitalist development.[37] But if the matter is put in a form to suggest that the contemporary world-system derives directly from the monopoly stage of the system's development, then we feel obliged to ask whether the monopoly stage itself does not derive from the earlier phase(s) of capitalism. Since it does, our argument is that the monopoly stage is by all means important, but not necessarily as important as the earlier phase(s) to which it owes itself.

But, then, while within Marxist circles the attention is confined to the problem of whether imperialism is an endemic part of capitalism or an added option, it is concentrated on capitalism of societies and away from the capitalist world-system.[38] The two approaches obviously have symbiotic relations with each other, but history seen from the world plane seems to support the assertion by Cox that "the sequence of motivation has been predominantly from system to societies."[39] The point to note is that if capital is that critical to the maturation of capitalism in Europe, as the Marxist model holds it is, and if we decide not to analyse a closed system, as Marx did, but to open this system at its world scale, then it becomes clear that, at the world-system level, the importance of *accumulated capital* translates into the importance of the *process of accumulation of capital on the world scale.*

From this perspective, it should not be too difficult to concede that externalization of capitalism has been around in *various forms* for as long as capitalism has been around in various forms. In short, as capitalism has changed in the course of its history, so have the forms of imperialism. And from this perspective we cannot hastily dismiss the prehistory of capital's external expression as sheer plunder, or sheer colonialism, because the making of world-history began with such prehistorical expressions of capital in evolution, no matter how illustrious it might now look to some. The point in history then becomes not so much whether imperialism is a policy or an endemic part of the capitalist form. The point becomes that capitalism, since its very beginning, has been expansive, and still is; and that the structural deformities which we see in the world today are the continuing products of capitalist expansionism, in pursuit of capital accumulation in the central formations and away from the peripheral formations.

The notion of social evolution, for all it may not tell us, tells us very clearly that "contexts of conjunctures" form watersheds in history. There are, of course, smaller watersheds within larger ones. So that while the whole of social evolution is clearly not a matter to be unravelled easily, the fact of the matter is that some historical changes are more profound than others. Some changes in fact have significance not so much in themselves as in the start they give to other and subsequent changes. As much as this is true, it also points to the fact that what one considers a major watershed, as distinct from a minor one, depends a great deal on what one's concerns and perspectives are.

Our perspective is the world-system, as an evolutionary unit; and our concern is the use of history to understand underdevelopment. So that we hold that even though in its history, capital accumulation has seen many changes, none of these changes can claim, or should be made to claim, to be more important than the very genesis of this history, because the beginning of this history was held to be the key to the endemic implications for the world as a whole; and because the determined present is best understood by reference to the very start of this history.[40]

If it is true, that what one considers a major watershed, as distinct from a minor one, depends a great deal on what one's concern and perspective are, then it is true that Marxists incurably find the so-called new imperialism of the nineteenth century more of a watershed than the initial spread of capitalist forces in the age of "discovery" and plunder, which interfered irreversibly with the lives of non-Europeans, because Marxists worship accumulated capital to the neglect of the initial processes of its accumulation. They underplay the similarities between the earlier and the later experiences of the accumulation process from the very beginning, because Marxism has (or shall we say some Marxists have) yet to benefit from any sustained world-system interpretations. The hostilities which have greeted the works of Baran, Sweezy, Frank, Amin, and Wallerstein, among others, are proof enough of this assertion.[41]

From our perspective, what is more striking about capitalism is its ability (since its emergence in the fifteenth century in Western Europe, when all areas of the world were "equal" in that they were all suffering from "feudal crises" of one kind or another)[42] to build the slight edge that Western Europe had into the larger disparity between the centre and the periphery of our world today.[43] Throughout the entire history of the world-capitalist *formation*, what has been the definitive essence of the centre-periphery relations has been the "terms of determining social actions," as Wallerstein puts it. The *motive* has been the transfer of valuables and values from the periphery to the centre. And the *mechanism* has been the exploitation-intended domination of the periphery by the centre, through the undeniable expansive real history of capitalism.

The decisive concern of most Marxists was, and continues to be, the conflict between the bourgeoisie and the proletariat in the centre countries. But gradually this concern is being shifted to the centre-periphery arena. As Sweezy says, in an allied vein of thought, "Concomitantly, and logically, the locus of creative marxist thought in economics as in other fields is shifting from the centre to the periphery."[44] This is to be hoped for, if it will move Marxists from their Eurocentric perch to a world-system view.

Some Marxist Concessions to the Eurocentric Charge

While most Marxists still cling to Lenin's Eurocentric conception of imperialism in its strictly technical sense, as the monopoly stage of capitalism, some contemporary Marxists, who count themselves among orthodox Marxists, have become acutely conscious of the rumblings of the Eurocentric charge and the encroaching need for a world-system frame of reference. Bob Sutcliffe is one such Marxist. To be sure, any concessions one can detect do not come about easily, because Lenin's position is held with so much respect that it is still considered as an explanation of "the genesis of imperialist war (the First World War),"[45] and as the "theory of the origins and drives of imperialism."[46] The concession to the need for the world-system view is made to appear as though it is appropriate only for the post-colonial dependency phase of imperialism as it pertains to multinational dominance. Despite all this, one can see that it is a brave attempt to reconcile the Marxist view of the subject with the world-system perspective, and its demonstrable continuity of imperialism thesis.

Sutcliffe is aware that Lenin's theory is nowadays often criticized on the grounds of its Eurocentricity, in that by "stressing the impulses to imperialism in the advanced capitalist countries it is claimed that he said too little about the changes wrought by imperialism in peripheral economies and societies."[47] This accusation, Sutcliffe believes, is unfair, for, as he says in another place, "The common accusations that Lenin's theory of imperialism is Eurocentric arise from a failure to consider [the implicit part of Lenin's theory dealing with the development in backward countries, backward Russia, that is]."[48]

Sutcliffe is also aware that the problem of definition is closely allied to that of historical timing or periodization. Further, he is aware that some argue that "imperialism always existed" and that others claim that nothing much changed in the objectives and methods of imperialism between the eighteenth century and the First World War. It is these reasons which encourage us to believe that what Sutcliffe says in response to the criticisms betrays some sensitivity to the Eurocentric charge, implies a recognition of the need for a world-system view, and amounts to a reasonable concession to the plausibility of our continuity of imperialism thesis. He writes:

> Now within Marxist writing on the subject there are, I think, three quite distinct phases (defined logically rather than temporally) in the relations between capitalism and the peripheral countries and areas of the world. One (prominent in Marx's and Engels' writing) involves plunder (of wealth or slaves) and exports of capitalist manufactures to the peripheral countries. The second (upper-most in Lenin's writing) involves the export of capital, competition for supplies of raw material and the growth of monopoly. The third involves a more complex, post-colonial dependency of the peripheral countries, in which [international corporations and unequal exchange] all play a role in confining, distorting or halting economic development and industrialization.

> In each of these phases of the imperialist relationship the peripheral areas furnish the needs of a capitalism whose home is in the advanced countries....

> Of course, it is not enough to think in terms of national capitalisms, since capitalism does move, though unevenly, toward becoming a world-system. This probably means that in the third phase in particular any idea of a national capitalist imperialism needs to be modified greatly.[49]

These are the elements of the concessions. In the first part of the quote, Sutcliffe strings together three distinct phases of imperialism, and by so doing he pushes whatever the phenomenon is meant to be to cover the plunder of wealth and slavery phase(s) of the development of capitalism. It ceases to be the property of any particular phase, and more importantly, it ceases to have meaning only in the frozen circumstances of certain late nineteenth century European variables.

In the second part of the quote, Sutcliffe concedes that each of the three distinct phases, including the earlier phase, contributed to the development of capitalism in Europe. In other words, the needs of

European capitalism, including capital accumulation in its prehistory or primary phase, were aided by imperialism; that is, European capitalism has involved the world from its very beginning to its present stage.

This is precisely the substance and the essence of the continuity of imperialism thesis. We now begin to approach "capitalist" imperialism, just as the thesis demands, as a sort of "rising" continuum which parallels the "rising" continuum of capitalist development, all through its history. It is now easy to see that as capitalism changed, so would imperialism.[50] It is now possible to see (capitalist) imperialism as a definite property of capitalism, and to proceed to reason that to the extent that capitalism in evolution differs from other modes of production, its "externalization," or its parasitic use of the "world," would differ from the parasitic use of the "world" by other modes of production.[51]

It then becomes a minor and a subordinate, if not an entirely irrelevant, question to ask whether capitalism's internal, or inherent, contradictions make it expand. The main question becomes the simple historical question as to whether capitalism's historicity has involved the emerging world from its beginning, and if so, whether the theory of capitalist development is not merely the history of its development, just as Frank says it is, when he writes, "Theory is history."[52] It is only when we take capitalist imperialism to be what our thesis suggests it is, that we shall cease to be amazed at the reality of the developmental consequences of world capitalist development. For example, contemporary writings would fit into a pattern, and it would not be that revealing to discover, as Baran and Sweezy did, that "far from being an exporter of capital, [Standard Oil of New Jersey] is a large and consistent *importer* of capital into the United States."[53] This finding would hold no surprises, simply because, insofar as capitalist development has related to capital accumulation, capital has always deserted the periphery for the centre.

If Lenin and other Marxists put "export of capital at the very centre of the economic stage," they were only using Eurocentric blinds to conceal the "world-truth" of the matter that, in the *fishing season*, anglers use small fishes to catch by far bigger ones.[54] The monopoly stage of capitalism was a fishing season *par excellence*. Some capital had to flee to the right parts of the world (does it matter whether it fled to the older colonies or the newer ones?) in order to return more capital.

In the third part of the quotation above, Sutcliffe appears very reluctant to concede the argument to the world-system perspective. He makes it appear that it is only in the third phase of imperialism that we may *probably greatly modify* any idea of a national capitalist imperialism in favour of a world capitalist system. There is no need for such hesitancy on Sutcliffe's part. It is true that capitalism did (and does) move unevenly towards becoming more and more of a world-system. But is it not also true that this movement, no matter how uneven, has progressed from an "unformed" to a "formed" state, as the capitalist world-system became more and more independent?[55] There is no doubt that national capitalism was in the ascendency at times and during periods of the development of capitalism, but this does not in any way deny the development of the capitalist system at the world-level. It does not argue against the development of the world-system from the earliest stages of capitalism, nor the mutual relationship between capitalism and imperialism.

It is, therefore, and indeed, true that "strictly speaking it is not possible to have a Marxist theory of imperialism, but only to look at imperialism as an aspect of the theory of capitalism."[56] As an aspect of capitalist development, Sutcliffe suggests that there are three concerns of imperialism. These are: (1) the development and the economic class structure of advanced capitalist societies (especially the factors which drive them towards geographical expansion of their economies) and the relations between them; (2) the economic and political relations between advanced nations and backward or colonial nations within the world capitalist system; and (3) the development of the economic and class structure in the more backward nations of the capitalist system, especially the root of their domination and their failure to industrialize.[57] He adds further that "a good deal of Marxist writing tries in principle to take these three concerns together and to construct a theory of the whole capitalist system. But the balance between them has shifted frequently."[58]

This much is true. And as much as it is, other observations are true, too. We shall make only two such observations, since full treatment of this matter will be undertaken elsewhere.[59] The first is that Marxists have shifted frequently because they have not paid the kind of heed they should have paid to the persistence of imperialism thesis; and the second is that in their treatment of the third concern (i.e., [3] above), in particular, they have been Eurocentric, and this has led them to pose the wrong questions with respect to capitalist development in the periphery. It will suffice for the moment to say that Marxists, when they take up the three concerns, have tended to see (2) and (3) above as the dependent variables with (1) as the independent variable. So long as this is done, the wrong questions will be posed with respect to (3), for the questions will always be shadowed by the silent Eurocentric question as to why the periphery is not like the centre; a Eurocentric perception of the world forms the basis of reasoning.

The continuity of imperialism and the world-system perspective would suggest that in order to give the Marxist theory of imperialism a coherence and a personality all its own, (1) and (3) above should be seen in terms of (2). From this perspective, we are then able to explain (1) and (3) in the dynamic terms of the relations between the advancing (as different from the advanced) nations and the non-advancing (as different from backward) nations within the development of the capitalist world-system.

From this viewpoint, we impose the dynamic imprint of process on the Marxist theory of uneven development to make a world-system property of the phenomenon which Frank has called "the development of underdevelopment," and for which phrase he has been endlessly maligned. For we shall see that it is not possible to accept that "the value of Frank's analysis is his magisterial critique of supposedly dual structure of peripheral societies,"[60] and then proceed to reject his "development of underdevelopment" thesis for being deterministic, as Palma does. If the critique is valid for societies, it is also valid for the world society. And if adherents of the world-system view are admonished (as they are in Palma's prize-winning essay, for example) for not accepting that "capitalist development takes place *on its own terms*, 'warts and all,'"[61] then they, in their turn, can ask whether what capitalist development has produced in the periphery is merely the blemish of warts or whether it is the much more serious disease, which Amin has diagnosed as "peripheral capitalist formation" and which Wallerstein has described as "the limited possibilities of transformation." This way, we approach the "internal" and the "external" debate not in terms of either-or, but in terms of their country and culture specifics, without prejudice to the abiding wholesomeness of the world-system and its common meaning to and for the periphery.

Notes

1. Gabriel Palma, "Dependency: A Formal Theory of Underdevelopment or a Methodology for the Analysis of Concrete Situations of Underdevelopment?" *World Development* 6 (July–August 1978): 888.
2. Palma (see note 1 above), p. 887.
3. E.M. Winslow, *The Pattern of Imperialism: A Study in Theories of Power* (Octagon Press, New York, 1972), p. 116.

4. Winslow (see note 3 above), p. 116.
5. The relevant references are in volume 1 of *Capital.*
6. Winslow (see note 3 above), p. 116.
7. Palma (see note 1 above), pp. 884–885.
8. See V.I. Lenin, *Imperialism: The Highest Stage of Capitalism* (International Publishers, New York, 1969); R. Luxemburg, *The Accumulation of Capital* (Routledge and Kegan Paul, London, 1963); Rudolf Hilferding, *Das Finanzkapital: Eine Studie über die jüngste Entwicklung des Kapitalismus* (Finance Capital: A Study of the Most Recent Development of Capitalism) (Brand, Vienna, 1910); Otto Bauer, *Die Nationalitätenfrage und die Sozialdemokratie* (Marx-Studien, Vienna, 1907); K. Kautsky, "Ultra-Imperialism," *New Left Review* 59 (Jan.–Feb. 1970); and also see the prescience of the world-system conception in Nikolai Bukharin, *Imperialism and World Economy* (Merlin Press, London, 1976).
9. Michael Barratt Brown, "A Critique of Marxist Theories of Imperialism," in R. Owen and B. Sutcliffe, eds., *Studies in the Theory of Imperialism* (Longman, London, 1972), p. 57. See also his *After Imperialism* (Heinemann, London, 1970).
10. This is the well-known argument of Lenin (see note 8 above), p. 63.
11. Lenin (see note 8 above), p. 88.
12. Lenin (see note 8 above), p. 88.
13. Lenin (see note 8 above), pp. 88–89.
14. Lenin (see note 8 above), p. 89.
15. S. Amin, *Accumulation on a World Scale: A Critique of the Theory of Underdevelopment*, vol. 1 (Monthly Review Press, New York, 1974), pp. 39–40.
16. Tom Kemp, "The Marxist Theory of Imperialism," in Owen and Sutcliffe (see note 9 above), pp. 17–18.
17. The distinction between the two holds interest only in strictly defined contexts.
18. We shall encounter this view from Sutcliffe, "Imperialism and Industrialization in the Third World," in Owen and Sutcliffe (see note 9 above), p. 172, again later in this chapter.
19. Sutcliffe (see note 18 above), p. 172.
20. Palma (see note 1 above), p. 903. Emphasis is Palma's.
21. These situations included: Russian development, the Narodnik interference with "pure Marxist thought," the vexing matters relating to the when, the how, and the where of the "impending" collapse of capitalism and the transition to socialism, the outbreak of the First World War and the workers' unexpected support for it, and the renegade but dangerously forceful voices of assorted leaders of the Second International and "a multitude of socialists, reformers, pacifists, bourgeois democrats and priests."
22. I owe a lot of what follows on Lenin's writing to a discussion I had with Johan Galtung at the UNU-GPID meeting in Geneva, 2–8 October 1978.
23. H. Magdoff, *The Age of Imperialism* (Monthly Review Press, New York, 1969), p. 5.
24. G. Arrighi, *The Geometry of Imperialism: The Limits of Hobson's Paradigm* (NLB, London, 1978), p. 19. For Arrighi's suggested interpretation of Lenin on imperialism, see pp. 10–11.
25. T. Kemp, "The Marxist Theory of Imperialism," in Owen and Sutcliffe (see note 9 above), p. 28.
26. Kemp (see note 25 above), p. 16.
27. See E. Williams, *Capitalism and Slavery* (University of North Carolina Press, Chapel Hill, N.C., 1944), for some of the early monopolies in the slave and sugar industries in the West Indies.
28. P.A. Baran, *The Political Economy of Growth* (Modern Reader Paperbacks, New York, 1968), p. 138.
29. Baran (see note 28 above), p. 138.

30. This is a crucial matter for our thesis.
31. Amin (see note 15 above), p. 22.
32. Amin (see note 15 above), p. 41.
33. D.W. Brogan, "Introduction" to Williams (see note 27 above), p. v.
34. Williams (see note 27 above), p. 210.
35. Williams (see note 27 above), p. 211.
36. See his *Unequal Development: An Essay on the Social Formations of Peripheral Capitalism* (Harvester Press, Sussex, 1976).
37. I owe this need to clarify my argument to Samir Amin's comments on an earlier draft. What follows in this section is an attempt to strengthen the credibility of my argument.
38. This point is very crucial in the world-system argument.
39. O.C. Cox, *Capitalism as a System* (Monthly Review Press, New York, 1964), p. x.
40. See note 37 above.
41. For the nature of the debate see: Ernesto Laclau, "Feudalism and Capitalism in Latin America," *New Left Review* 67 (1971); A. Emmanuel, *Unequal Exchange: A Study of the Imperialism of Trade* (MRP, London, 1972), pp. 271–431; Ernesto Laclau, *Politics and Ideology in Marxist Theory* (NLB, London, 1977), pp. 15–50; A.G. Frank, *World Accumulation, 1492–1789* (Macmillan, London, 1978), pp. 238–271; I. Wallerstein, *The Capitalist World-Economy* (Cambridge University Press, Cambridge, 1979), pp. 138–151; R. Brenner, "Dobb on the Transition from Feudalism to Capitalism," *Cambridge Journal of Economics* 2 (1978): 121–140; R. Brenner, "Reply to Sweezy," *New Left Review* 108 (March–April 1978); and R. Brenner, "The Origins of Capitalist Development: A Critique of Neo-Smithian Marxism," *New Left Review* 104 (1977): 25–93.
42. In particular, see Laclau, *Politics and Ideology in Marxist Theory* (note 41 above), pp. 15–50.
43. Baran (see note 28 above), p. 137.
44. I. Wallerstein, *The Modern World-System: Capitalist Agriculture and the Origins of European World Economy in the Sixteenth Century* (Academic Press, New York, 1974), p. 72.
45. Paul Sweezy, "Marxian Economics," *Monthly Review* 7 (1976): 6.
46. Sutcliffe (see note 18 above), p. 172.
47. Sutcliffe (see note 18 above), p. 174.
48. Sutcliffe (see note 18 above), p. 172.
49. Sutcliffe, "Conclusion," in Owen and Sutcliffe (see note 9 above), p. 321.
50. Sutcliffe (see note 18 above), pp. 172–173.
51. The parallel changes mentioned here cover both secular and cyclical changes in capitalism.
52. M.I. Finley, "Empire in the Graeco-Roman World," *Review* 2 (1978): 55–68, lends support for this position.
53. Paul A. Baran and Paul Sweezy, "Notes on the Theory of Imperialism," in K.T. Fann and Donald C. Hodges, eds., *Readings in U.S. Imperialism* (Porter Sargent, Boston, 1971), p. 75.
54. There is a Ghanaian saying which goes: "Ye de nam na eyi nam." It means, "We use smaller fishes to catch larger ones."
55. Sutcliffe (see note 49 above), p. 320.
56. Sutcliffe (see note 49 above), p. 320.
57. Sutcliffe (see note 49 above), p. 320.
58. Sutcliffe (see note 49 above), p. 320.
59. See my "A Third World View of the World-System Methodology" (Mimeo, 1980).
60. Palma (see note 1 above), p. 899.
61. Palma (see note 1 above), p. 912.

Part Three

A World-System Basis for a Theory of Imperialism

Chapter Six

The Thesis

The Continuity of Imperialism Thesis

In this chapter, we present the essence of the continuity of imperialism thesis and, by so doing, return to aspects of the world-system methodology in order to situate the *thesis* firmly in its tradition.

Our insistence all along has been on the primary inclusion of the "world" as an evolving unit, the world-system, in the accumulation of capital business, from its very beginning. What we have proposed, therefore, is that in the process of understanding in its totality the process of accumulating capital in Europe and away from the rest of the world, we should not consider any part of the world, no matter how dominating it may be, or might have been, at any time within the capitalist historicity, as more important than the "world" as a whole.

This conception of imperialism differs from the Eurocentric liberal, radical, and Marxist conceptions, in that it considers imperialism in the *specific* and *total* context of the history of the methodical and persistent accumulation of capital in Europe from its very nascence in the fifteenth century to the present.

It sees imperialism from the point of view of the continuity of the involvement of the non-European world in the evolving "world" in terms of the cost implications that this evolving "world" patterned for the non-European world.

The exact point of departure is, therefore, *four-squarely based on the distinction we refuse to make between the earlier history of the process of capital accumulation, the so-called prehistory of capital, and the world-history consequences of capital as an already accumulated thing, dating from the emergence of finance capital in Europe in the late nineteenth century.*

The continuity of imperialism thesis, then, is based firmly on the refusal to consider the difference between the so-called "old" and "new" imperialisms as qualitative. To accept that this difference was qualitative would go against the world-system postulates. We concede that there was a difference between the "old" and the "new" imperialisms. The difference meant, among other things, the final push by European powers to complete the division of the world among themselves, and the destruction of free competition by the concentration and the centralization of capital in finance capital monopolies. We concede further that the difference was due to some changes in European societies, and that in the limited context of Europe, these changes may have been qualitative. What we do not concede, however, is the sharp distinction that other conceptions of imperialism make between the old and the new capitalist forms of imperialism. We reject this distinction not because it did not occur but because no matter how sharp the distinction may have appeared to Eurocentrics, if and when the unit of analysis becomes the evolving world-system, the distinction turns out not to be *qualitative* but merely *the acceleration of the earlier processes.*

Hodgkin, in his review of the few existing non-European "consumer" theories of imperialism, showed that these theories tended to see the imperialist phenomenon as a process beginning with the earliest periods of the capitalist novelty. And we, for our part, have attempted, through the review of European "producer" theories of imperialism, to show that the continuity of the imperialist experience can be sustained, if the phenomenon is approached from the world-system perspective. We have endeavoured to show that producer theorists, in their Eurocentric haste to define the concept of imperialism, have been reckless in their periodization of the historical concept imperialism within the capitalist historicity; and, for this reason, they have been either *imprecise* or *over-precise* in their dating of this unique experience of the world as a definite system.

We pointed out, with respect to the Marxist view of the subject, that the hindrance to its appreciation of the continuity of imperialism thesis appeared to be that the Eurocentric terms of reference in the Marxist mode of thought do not compel Marxist theorists to see the imperialist phenomenon in a coherent and continuous historical manner, from the point of view of the impact of capitalist expansion on both Europe and the rest of the world from the very beginning of the history of capitalism. But while the Marxist conception of imperialism continues to be Eurocentric, a few writers within the Marxist camp have attempted seriously to compensate for the glaring lack of world-system perspective by introducing world-history as the theory to understand the present. These are the writers I have referred to above in connection with world-system methodology. These writers have been called Third Worldist, Circulationists, Smithians, and Neo-Marxist by other Marxists,[1] who consider the attempts to include non-Europeans in world-history and the emphasis on the capitalist world-system as a unit distinct from and containing competing national capitalisms as tantamount to heretic interference with the much-cherished conventional Eurocentric assumptions in the theory of capital accumulation. This is most unbecoming of the followers of the critical thinker that Marx was.

It must be pointed out that in some circles, where the Marxist mode of thought is held in high respect, the need for a world-system perspective is being advocated with honest conviction.[2] The works of these writers may differ in their character, and they may not all focus specifically on the same questions relating to the grand details of the origins of world-history, but, as I indicated in the early chapters, heuristically and historiographically, they have a lot in common.[3] In this tradition of thought, no disrespect is intended for Marxist mode of thought. On the contrary, it is meant to up-date its relevance for our times.

Now, let us advance the discussion of the *thesis* via a reference to Wallerstein's presentation of the epochs in world capitalist history. Wallerstein sees the history of capitalism as falling into roughly the following four major epochs:
— 1450–1640, the origins and the early conditions of the world-system;
— 1640–1815, the consolidation period for this system;
— 1815–1917, the period of "the conversion of the world-economy into a global enterprise, made possible by the technological transformation of modern industrialism"; and
— 1917 to the present, a period for the further consolidation of the capitalist world-economy, a consolidation in a deeper sense than the earlier 1640–1815 consolidation phase.[4]

Visiting our continuity of imperialism thesis on Wallerstein's major epochs, we see that the first epoch was indeed "still only a European world-system," in that the very early phase saw Europe turning on itself to exploit the European ecology — the European frontier[5] — the Americas and the Caribbean Islands;[6] and by the end of this epoch, Europe could not conceive of itself without the Americas. And, more profoundly, the Americas would never be the same again; their histories had been allotted roles in the evolving European world-economy — world-history. By the middle of this period the slave trade was on, and there was no mistaking what it represented — good business. By the end of the period the "world" for Europe had ceased to be Europe's old stomping grounds of the Middle and the Near-Far East and the northern coasts of Africa.[7] The second epoch may have been a period of consolidation for the system's European home-base, but this consolidation cannot be considered without the incorporated areas outside Europe, and certainly the consolidation did not mean the abandonment of further incorporation of, and penetration into, areas in Africa and Asia. The conversion epoch of 1815–1917 was rapid in accomplishing its mission, and very thorough at that. But the speed and the thoroughness of accomplishment could not have been possible had it not been for the *prior* expansive penetration and effective construction of bridgeheads in most of the places involved. This conversion phase owes a lot to the maturation of capital, which aided the technological transformation Wallerstein refers to. But long before the maturation of concentrated capital, the future of the non-European world had been settled in the Americas, Australia, New Zealand, and other parts; and for the "newly" incorporated, their subordinate role in this global enterprise was assured.

It bears stating that it was during the terminal phase of this third epoch, when the "world-wideness" of the economy was solidly and fully achieved, that it became convenient and fashionable for the different Eurocentrics — anti-capitalist theorists, radical reformers, and capitalist apologetics — to see the externalization of the system — imperialism — as a phenomenon of their times.

The Capitalist-Imperialist Phase Relationships

If capitalist expansion is the carrier of the world-historical matter of our time, what is the defining characteristic of this history? It is the "unequal development in a multilayered format of layers within layers, each one polarized in terms of a bimodal distribution of rewards,"[8] from the highest top to the lowest bottom, a vicious interlocking system of chains of exploitation, each higher level feeding on siphoned surplus from levels lower than it. This is the legacy of history for our times. This is history as the present — a deformed complex of well-adjusted pyramidal networks of exploitation. The mark of our times, as Wallerstein sees it, is "the imagination of its profiteers and the counter assertiveness of the oppressed. Exploitation and the refusal to accept exploitation as either inevitable or just constitute the continuing antinomy of the modern era, joined together in a dialectic which has far from reached its climax in the twentieth century."[9]

For these reasons, we are inclined to believe that when we come to consider the *vastness* of the expansion of this new world formation, its *swiftness*, and the *thoroughness* of it, all made possible by the mind-boggling developments in technology, in comparison to the *limited, slow* and *not so thorough* expansions of earlier periods, we are compelled to expose the falseness of similarities which the kindred nature of expansions could harbour, in presenting the two different expansions as the same. This is because we are not merely comparing old and new forms of the same phenomenon. The nature of the expansion that gave birth to the world-system and its history is very different from earlier and older practices and forms of expansion. For this reason, the concept imperialism, which we use to express this uniqueness, must be allowed to stand by itself; moreover, it must not be confused with any other attenuated conception, or stage, of world-history.

The so-called new imperialism, dating from the late nineteenth century, was both a consolidating exercise and a mopping-up operation for this qualitatively different expansion which began in the late fifteenth century. The world today derives a lot of its most prominent structural legacies and deformities from the history and the evolution of this expansion since at least the 1500s, the quickening of the deformities in the age of monopoly capitalism notwithstanding. It is for these reasons, which we believe amount to much more than a plea for semantic clarity with respect to the term *imperialism*, that, if we choose to refer to the process of global expansion of capitalism since the 1500s and its implications as *imperialist*, we should be careful to distinguish this particular kind of expansion from earlier expansions. We should not ascribe the same term uncritically and *imprecisely* to cover all expansions, as the liberals do, or *over-precisely* to cover only a particular stage of the capitalist expansion, as radicals and most Marxists do. The plea is that, when we come to examine the contemporary texture of the relations between nation-states, and within them, insofar as this texture is the product of world-history, we should endeavour to distinguish between immediately relevant and not so relevant influences of history.

According to the continuity of imperialism thesis, then, we view imperialism not so much as an endemic or an inherent property of capitalism, but as very simply *a fact of its history at the world-system level.* We can say, therefore, that if it is true that imperialism has been around in various forms at the level of the evolving world-system, ever since the initial emergence of capitalism in the late fifteenth century, then it ought to be clear that we cannot treat imperialism without reference to the changing tones of capitalism. Imperialism has no autonomous existence of its own; it can exist only with reference to the changing tones of capitalism in evolution. Imperialism is only descriptive of the world-system consequences of the evolution of the capitalist world-economy in pursuit of *efficient* means of accumulating capital; and, further, as capitalism and its needs become different, so will imperialism change.

From this, we can conceive a rough parallel phase-relationship between world capitalism and imperialism in the following manner:

Phases of World Capitalism	*Phases of Imperialism*
I. 1500s–1640s	
Initial explorations serving the foundations of the world-economy; early mercantilist form.	Plunder and incursions; some early white settlements and colonies in parts of evolving "world."
II. 1640s–1750s	
Consolidation of mercantilism in an evolving "world" context; outlines of world-system clear.	Plunder continues in other parts; colonies and white settlements continue; bridgeheads strengthening. Trade in substance and in "Pacotilles."
III. 1750s–1870s	
Classical capitalism, capital accumulated in Europe, from all over the world, matures in Europe; capital begets capital, primitive accumulation from parts of the world continues.	Colonialism continues but accelerates to cover "remote" parts of the world; the outlines of *dependency* of the periphery of the world-system on its centre now perceptible.
IV. 1870s–1950s	
Monopoly capitalism. "European" finance capital accelerates the capitalization of the world to produce	Maturing of *dependency*; granting of political independence for some; economic and other ties

more capital in "Europe" and away from "non-Europe." Primitive accumulation evolves into clear unequal exchange in trade and other relations.

ensuring periphery subordinate incorporation into the world-economy; early *neo-colonial* forms.

V. 1950s—Present

Transnational corporation (TNC) form emerges; capital becomes really centralized and concentrated in Europe, while paradoxically it is pervasive world-wide and, as a result, a *New International Division of Labour* (NIDL)[10] ensues.

Remaining colonies become independent; dependency develops in subtleties; *neo-colonialism*, the general mode of subordinating periphery to centre; and periphery élites consequently demand a *New International Economic Order* (NIEO) for tokenistic and ameliorative rewards,[11] for their Euro-centric imitations of development and their meek integration into the world-system and its system of élites.

This scheme does not, of course pretend to be the exact story of any particular part of the world. Different parts of the world experienced the effects of the capitalist world expansion at different times. For example, when the Latin American periphery was experiencing neo-colonialism, some parts of Africa and Asia were barely emerging from the plunder phase of imperialism. What we have sought to do in the scheme is to capture the ascent tones of the evolving world-economy and their corresponding imperialist phases, at the periods indicated. In this regard, we must surely recall what Baran wrote: "... in attempting to comprehend the laws of motion of both the advanced and the backward parts of the capitalist world, it is possible and indeed mandatory to abstract from peculiarities of the individual cases and to concentrate on their common essential characteristics."[12]

According to the continuity of imperialism thesis, the message in the above scheme is that the imperialist phenomenon has taken different forms with the evolving tones of world capitalism, but that the imperialist experiences of the imperialized parts of the world show a continuity, irrespective of the changing forms that imperialism assumes as capitalism itself changes. The continuity of the experiences is to be understood in terms of the persistence of exploitation of the periphery by the centre in aid of accumulating capital in the centre and away from the periphery. The emphasis here is on the persistence and the graduating subtlety of exploitation.

With specific reference to the conception of imperialism within the world-system tradition, Wallerstein, Hopkins, and the Braudel Centre appear to have approached the subject on one occasion as a matter in passing while presenting a summary of the world-system methodology; and on another occasion, Wallerstein approached it as a matter for some specific, even if brief, deliberation.

On the first occasion, Wallerstein and Hopkins, and the Braudel Centre approached the subject this way:

> The reality of imperium is as old as recorded history. The term itself derives from Roman usage. What might be called its neo-Roman usage derives from its association in the mid-nineteenth century with Napoleon III. Its contemporary usage, as a phenomenon particular to the capitalist world-economy, is derived from Hobson and Lenin.... [Both politician and scholar] have been moved to argue that the end of direct colonial rule has meant the end of imperialism. They have used the locution of "neo-colonialism" to describe the continuing ability of core states to interfere politically in the economic activities of peripheral states. On the other hand, scholars, [who had the nineteenth century experiences in mind] have noted that imperial interests were best pursued without the imposition of direct colonial rule. They have termed this phenomenon "informal empire." If we use the term "imperialism" to refer to any use of political power by a stronger state ... against a weaker state intended to alter allocations in the world market, either directly or indirectly, then it is easy to maintain that this is a constant of the inter-state system as it has operated within the capitalist world-economy. We could then view "informal empire" and "colonialism" as cyclical alternatives in the form of imperialism.[13]

We can begin to see the continuity of imperialism thesis alluded to towards the end of the quote. But by referring to the age of the "reality of imperium," the authors were calling our attention to the etymology of the concept. Such a reference, however, runs the unintended risk of falling into the Eurocentric liberal imprecision. The authors are correct in associating contemporary usage of the concept imperialism with Hobson and Lenin. But such an association could be potentially dangerous, as it

124

could move us too closely towards the rigid radical and Marxist Eurocentric *over-precise* use of the term to describe a stage in the effects of the development of "European" capitalism on the world. The reference to "neo-colonialism" and "informal empire" only alerts us to the variations within the effects on the world during and since the maturation of capital in Europe.

It is when the authors use the term imperialism to refer to *any* use of political power for the intended purpose of altering allocations in the world market that we must refer to the danger of seeing imperialism, in the terms that are too similar to the manner in which the liberals appreciate it, as a phenomenon of political *means*, and not as a phenomenon related to a specific economic *theme*.[14] We say this because our discussion of imperialism, as a historical concept, demanded precise historical specificity for imperialism, in order to distinguish it from falsely kindred terms. Our particular understanding of the world-system frame would insist that imperialism can take any form in means — political, economic, military, or cultural, or any combination of them — but that this is not the main distinguishing feature of the term, within the world-system identity. The historic uniqueness of the concept imperialism, within this frame, resides in the historic identity of its *theme*, accumulation of capital, of which allocations in the world market are an indelible functional expression, and of whose means the political is only one.

In our view, the changing *means* associated with imperialism are of interest only insofar as they refer to the constancy of the *theme* of accumulating capital in parts of the world, and, by implication, away from others. Cyclical variations are no doubt of great interest within the world-system frame. They refer to probably repeating patterns of change over "short" or "long" periods during the capitalist world-economy. Such changes no doubt can affect aspects of imperialist relations in the economy. However, it is within the thrust of the secular trend of the accumulation of capital on a "world" scale that the concept imperialism acquires its full historical and analytic bloom, embracing the significance of the cyclical changes within the world-economy. In our view, therefore, it would appear that it is very similar to the liberal view of imperialism to align the identity of imperialism too closely with *means*. For, if seen as such, it is easy to "maintain that this is a constant of the interstate system as it has operated within the capitalist world-economy," and it becomes equally easy to maintain, as Koebner and other liberals do, that as a means of influencing market allocations, imperialism is as old as human history. Such a view, however, loses sight, even temporarily, of the need for the term's relevant historical specificity. Admittedly, the two arguments are miles apart. But given the characteristic fluidity of liberal arguments, liberals can easily argue that "states" have been around for a long time and, therefore, so have the interstate system and imperialism.

The second occasion when Wallerstein approached the concept imperialism within the world-system methodology, as a matter for some deliberation, he was unfortunately too brief, but characteristically to the point. This second approach indicates that perhaps Wallerstein, and the Braudel Centre, were aware of some of the points raised above. The change in perspective is supportive of the continuity of imperialism thesis.

Wallerstein begins his essay with a bold reference to the two senses in which our current concepts are time bound, and from our perspective, therefore, Eurocentric.[15] He argues that by stressing what is said to be "*new* in the capitalist world-economy after 1870, Hobson and Lenin have seriously misled us. They have separated capitalism and imperialism into two separate phenomena, leading us to construe imperialism as a 'stage' of capitalist development, as a *foreign policy* of given states at given points of time. This diagnosis has led to two prognoses, neither of which has worked."[16]

Much more to the point, Wallerstein states that "imperialism has ranges from its familiar, contemporary neo-colonial form of World Bank loan requirements to the 'export of capital' chasing after cheaper labour as observed by Hobson and Lenin to the plunder of the buccaneers in the seventeenth century Caribbean."[17]

Even if Wallerstein's arguments appear to point to imperialism as a cyclical phenomenon,[18] while ours ride more on the secular identity of the world-economy, the similarity between the two essays should move us nearer to Oliver Cox's view that imperialism has been an abiding attribute of capitalism.[19]

Another work which also appears to support the thesis is Ranjit Sau's book on imperialism.[20] In this work, Sau argues that imperialism is not just a late stage of capitalism but something much more fundamental than that.

We should not really be surprised at the similar positions taken by these works, for they attempted to do no more than draw theoretical refinements of the concept of imperialism from the conceptual richness of the world-system perspective. This should alert us to the fact that, in its early period, this approach to political economy may appear conceptually rich but theoretically poor.[21] This need not be so. The theoretical sophistication of this perspective cannot be demonstrated beyond doubt by the refinement of only one concept, however. For this to be so, many more concepts deserve such refinements.

As we stated in an earlier chapter, one refined concept should lead to other refined concepts, if analyses of social and historical phenomena are not to stagnate, and if we are to uncover hidden relationships of great importance for an understanding of our world and its transformation.

Among other immediate concepts, *capitalism, development*, and *exploitation*, and how they relate to imperialism, deserve urgent consideration from the world-system perspective, if we are to rescue the ideas usually associated with *development* from the bindings of earlier times.

Finally, I shall say that the continuity of imperialism thesis, as advanced here, may be seen by some as "third worldist." This is (perhaps) true. And while I ordinarily would object to "third worldisms" for their own sakes, in the face of the entrenched Eurocentric conceptions of imperialism, such an interpretation of world-history is not to be deplored, provided it can help in tilting the balance towards a world-view for the important purpose of a better understanding of our contemporary world and its transformation.

A much more interesting question to raise at this point is: Why the emphasis on the continuity of imperialism? The simple answer is, that in establishing the continuity of imperialism thesis, we are forced to confront the need for investigating where its dynamics and the vitalities lie at this phase of world-history. We touch on this important matter in chapter seven.

Notes

1. See the references in note 41 of chapter five.
2. I refer to the world-system adherents discussed earlier.
3. For a discussion on some of the methodological differences between these and some other writers, see my "World System or World-System? The Historiographic Significance of a Hyphen" (Mimeo, 1980).

4. Immanuel Wallerstein, *The Modern World-System: Capitalist Agriculture and the Origins of the European World Economy in the Sixteenth Century* (Academic Press, New York, 1974), pp. 10–11.

5. Wallerstein (see note 4 above), p. 5.

6. Immanuel Wallerstein, "The Caribbean and the Capitalist World-Economy in the Seventeenth Century," *Caribbean Yearbook of International Relations* (Sijthoff, The Hague, 1978).

7. Eric Williams, *From Columbus to Castro: The History of the Caribbean 1492–1969* (Andre Deutsch, London, 1978), p. 13.

8. Wallerstein (see note 4 above), p. 64.

9. Wallerstein (see note 4 above), p. 239.

10. Folker Fröbel, Jürgen Heinrichs, and Otto Kreye, *The New International Division of Labour* (Cambridge University Press, London, 1980).

11. See my "Contemporary Adaptation Dialectic of the World Economic System: An Introductory Probing," *Caribbean Yearbook of International Relations* (Sijthoff, The Hague, 1976), pp. 439–463; and see also the essays in Herb Addo, ed., *Transforming the World-Economy? Nine Critical Essays on the New International Economic Order* (Hodder and Stoughton, London, 1984).

12. P.A. Baran, *The Political Economy of Growth* (Modern Reader Paperbacks, New York, 1968), p. 134.

13. Terence Hopkins and Immanuel Wallerstein, "Patterns of Development of the Modern World-System: Research Proposal," *Review* 1, no. 2:120–121.

14. See M.I. Finley, "Empire in the Graeco-Roman World," *Review* 2, no. 1 (1978): 55–68.

15. Wallerstein, "Imperialism and Development" (Mimeo, 1979), p. 1.

16. Wallerstein (see note 15 above), p. 7.

17. Wallerstein (see note 15 above), p. 10. See also note 6 above.

18. Wallerstein (see note 15 above), p. 10.

19. O.C. Cox, *Capitalism as a System* (Monthly Review Press, New York, 1964), p. 136.

20. Ranjit Sau, *Unequal Exchange, Imperialism and Underdevelopment: Essays on Political Economy of World Capitalism* (Oxford University Press, New Delhi, 1978).

21. This issue came up in the discussion of Pat McGowan's paper, "Problems of Theory and Data in the Study of World-System Dynamics," presented at the ISA 21st Annual Convention, Los Angeles, 18–22 March 1980. See T.K. Hopkins, "World-System Analysis: Methodological Issues," in B.H. Kaplan, ed., *Social Change in the Capitalist World Economy* (Sage Publications, London, 1978) as well as C. Chase-Dunn, "Comparative Research on World-System Characteristics," *International Studies Quarterly* 23, no. 4 (1979): 601–623.

Chapter Seven

The Crisis and Some Derivative Hypotheses

The Thesis and the Crisis in the Theory of Imperialism

As we can see from the preceding chapters, the concept imperialism has
come to mean all manner of things to Eurocentrics. It should not be too
surprising, therefore, if some seem to think that a sort of a crisis
equivalent to permanent revolution has crept into the theory of
imperialism. To Eurocentric liberals, the crisis is due to the fact that the
nebulous concept is over-used by the radicals and Marxists, who use it to
explain practically everything in international political economy; hence
the call by the Eurocentric liberals to excise the concept from serious
discourse.[1] But to the radicals and the orthodox Marxists,[2] the source of
the crisis is that, within its *over-precise* definitional boundary, the theory
of imperialism threatens to change its *very meaning* from crisis to crisis
within capitalism. To these latter groups of Eurocentrics, the crisis
problem is very serious, for it is not just that, like the chameleon, the
theory of imperialism merely changes its colour from one critical
situation in capitalism to another. It is that the curious situation exists
where the theory of imperialism threatens to change not just its colour, or
its form, but its very nature, from one critical point to another in the
evolution of capitalism, while, very strangely, it continues to bear the
same name.

The problem in this curious crisis is that there is no theoretically
consistent thread which explains and justifies why the same name should
be given to such different phenomena.

One writer who attempts to throw some light on why there is this sense
of permanent crisis in the Marxist theory of imperialism is Jonathan
Friedman.[3] He argues that all existing theories of imperialism "seem to
be descriptively adequate to the periods when they were conceived. But
they are clearly of limited application — limited to their immediate
historical situation."[4] Friedman senses something seriously wrong, when

129

he asks: "Can it be that Marxists, who have always attacked empiricism, have nonetheless created no more than so many empirical abstractions in lieu of genuine theoretical models?"[5] Friedman states that "at the moment we are in the midst of yet another crisis in imperialism theory — between those who hold fast to the hierarchical centre/periphery model and those who find that there is increasing capitalist development in the Third World."[6]

According to Friedman, the main problem in the crisis seems to be that "Marxists, just as non-Marxists, have attempted to relate their empirical situation directly to a fixed set of categories instead of attempting to revise the categories themselves, to discover theoretical schemes that might generate their immediate reality as well as other 'realities' past and future."[7]

Friedman goes on to make the point that because Marxists are not theoretically prepared, "every change in the real situation tends to come as a surprise"[8] to their theory of imperialism.

> Such situations, where theory and reality contradict one another, ought to lead as quickly as possible to the reconstitution of theory. Instead, it has most often led to a hardening of positions — usually reified by differing political standpoints. This in itself may help to distort attempts at explanation in such a way that we are sure to limit the relevance of our theories to particular historical situations that have become internalized as the definition of the "highest stage" of capitalism or of just plain capitalism in general.[9]

The unconstructive situation has arisen, therefore, where, according to Friedman, "TRUTH and the CORRECT LINE march hand in hand against the revisionists, deviationists, Trotskyists, bourgeois academics [not forgetting third worldists], etc."[10]

Indeed, there is a crisis in the theory of imperialism, but, from our perspective, it is a Eurocentric crisis which, therefore, must be left to Eurocentrics to resolve, if they can.

From our world-system perspective, there is no crisis in the theory of imperialism. We can confidently say that the coherence established by the continuity of imperialism thesis provides a connecting thread, which, properly handled, can remove the theory-situation gaps and rigidities in the theory of imperialism.

Any theory of imperialism based on our *thesis* will not allow the nature of the concept of imperialism to run conveniently after changing realities or ossify in the circumstances of a particular point in history. Instead, it will be theoretically prepared for "immediate reality as well as other 'realities' past and future."

On the nature of the crisis in the theory of imperialism, this is not the place to discuss the thesis of "increasing capitalist development in the Third World."[11] The idea of *development* in the third world and its relationship to the idea of *imperialism* in the context of capitalist history deserve separate consideration. In any such consideration, however, we cannot avoid beginning with the changing nature of centre-periphery relations throughout the history of capitalism.

The arguments here have long gone past whether there is a centre and a periphery in the world-system and its economy and what roles these parts play in the combined generation and in the competitive accumulation of capital. So that, if we begin with the centre and the periphery of the world-economy, the problem becomes the complex problem of how the centre is changing, how the periphery is changing, and how the links between the centre and the periphery themselves are changing, all in the changing context of the world-system totality. It is precisely this complex set of processes which Johan Galtung aptly describes as "a process with a centre and a periphery, both of them moving, the exact processes within them changing, but *the gradient of exploitation* remains, enriching the centre, impoverishing the periphery in various ways."[12]

This interrelating set of changing processes is complex;[13] and it must be respected as such, if we are to be sensitive to the "modern mythology of change," the extent to which, in our modern world, transformation, change, etc., have come to mean the reproduction of more of the same in superficially changing contexts, thus allowing things to remain essentially the same while they are said to have changed.[14]

This complexity is not beyond comprehension and action, once we break the bounds of Eurocentricity to reveal that world-history is not shaped by what goes on in the centre alone but also by what goes on in the periphery as well as what goes on between the two.

It is in the context of this complexity that orthodox Marxist thinking on imperialism, because of its Eurocentric nature, loses the subtle realism which should be its legacy. In fact, on the matter of imperialism, orthodox Marxist thinking stops altogether. The precise point of cessation is when orthodox Marxists have to relate the processes in the centre and in the periphery to the crucial linking processes which relate both changes to the exploitation of the periphery by the centre. As far as imperialism is concerned, the tradition in the orthodox Marxist theory is to stop exactly where it ought to begin. It understands imperialism wrongly as something done by European capital, at a stage in world-history, to non-European areas of the world. It does not understand imperialism's current form and effect as anything more than the reverberations of this earlier one-shot, one-stage, act in history. It is incapable of seeing imperialism as a continuous relational process linking the evolving periphery to the evolving centre since the dawn of world capitalism.

Let us recall parts of our criticism of Sutcliffe's presentation of the Marxist theory of imperialism in the last pages of chapter five. We stated there that the Marxist theory of imperialism views processes in the centre as the determining factors in the resulting processes between the centre and the periphery and in the periphery itself. We argued then that, for as long as this is done, the wrong question, as to why the periphery is not like the centre, will persist as a scientific query. This question, we suggested, was Eurocentric. And, for as long as it continues to be put, it will solicit theoretical and empirical works that are external to the realities in the periphery. It will invite Eurocentrically encouraging theoretical apologia and misleading Eurocentric empirical confidence-boosters. At best, it will invite more empirical works, claiming to be studying the "laws of motion" of capitalism and indicating that the periphery is not developing because it is being exploited by the centre. In all this, Marxists take the idea of development to mean industrialization; and underdevelopment, the absence of industrialization, is taken out of its historical-relational context to be the property of the periphery and not the property of the world-system, the history of which enabled parts to industrialize and make it impossible for other parts to do so. It may be that to regard industrialization as development, meaning essentially the efficient production of things by means of efficient exploitation of human and non-human resources, is itself Eurocentric. But that is another problem.

The present problem is the discussion of the extent to which concentrating on internal-centre processes denies the theory of imperialism the connecting link it needs for us to understand relevant past realities, explain present realities, and relate both to anticipate future "realities" in ways that are helpful to actions seeking to transform the world.

The continuity of imperialism thesis provides such a theoretically coherent thread in the world-system theory of imperialism, for, it alerts us to ask the question: Why has imperialism been so continuous, and successfully so? This question compels us to search for the forces that have been active in imperialism since its historic beginning. In the course of doing this, if we remember that imperialism is not something only sources in the centre societies do to the periphery, but something which some sources in the periphery also participate in, then we are led to two major sources of processes on which to base a world-system theory of imperialism. They are, at the first encounter: *internal-centre sources of imperialism and internal-periphery sources of imperialism.*

Once we do this, we begin to approach a world-system theory of imperialism, which sees the imperialism phenomenon as a world phenomenon from its beginning and which detects the dynamism in this phenomenon in terms of its very *continuity*, essentially the *continuities in the link between the internal-centre and the internal-periphery sources of imperialist relations.* The essence in such a theory is located in the two-way imperialist *link* between the imperialist processes in the centre and those in the periphery, that is, in the *evolving* centre capitalist process and in the *evolving* periphery capitalist processes, from the very beginning of world capitalism in evolution.

The coherence in this theory is provided by the fact that it sees imperialism in terms of the totality of social (economic, political, military, cultural, etc.) relations between the centre and the periphery within the capitalist world-system. As changes occur in the centre and/or in the periphery, so will the forms, not the nature, of the exploitative relations called imperialism also change to ensure the continuity of the exploitative essence of the relations, perhaps even to maintain the *constancy of the exploitation gradient.*

The admitted major problem in the Marxist theory of imperialism all along, according to Sutcliffe, has been that "a good deal of Marxist writing *tries in principle* to take these three concerns [internal-centre development, relations between the centre and the periphery, and internal-periphery developments] together and to construct a theory of the whole capitalist system. But the balance between them [the three concerns] *has shifted frequently*." (Emphases added.)[15]

133

The balance has shifted frequently because the Marxist theory erratically and fadishly runs after empirically time-specific concrete situations, within a truncated conception of the capitalist historicity, which are then abstracted into theories of imperialism without regard for the continuity links between these abstractions, called theories, all through capitalist history. Further, the balance has shifted, frequently and apologetically, for the reason that the Marxist theory of imperialism, Eurocentrically, seeks to explain internal-periphery and centre-periphery processes in terms of internal-centre processes.

To proceed, I must make a vital point absolutely clear. Seeing that our conception of the world-system theory of imperialism is four-squarely based on the continuity of imperialism thesis, I must state that *continuity*, as used here, means that the nature of imperialism, the historic meaning of imperialism, the historic role of imperialism *vis-à-vis* the historic theme of accumulating capital in the centre and away from the periphery, is a *continuous* historic phenomenon, connected, unbroken, and uninterrupted in its historic sequence within its historicity. Continuous does not mean constant or stagnant *sameness*. It means a changingness which keeps *sameness* in nature or essence intact, even though form and appearance may change.

The argument is that, at any one time, imperialism is to be understood as the relation(s) between two sets of real situations, two sets of realities, namely the capitalist developments in the centre and those in the periphery within the world capitalist system. This imperialist relation is itself a maturing process, refining its manner without changing its nature, as it matures. It is this maturing aspect of imperialism which explains at once the subtlety and the persistence of the exploitation of the periphery by the centre in the continuous history of world capitalism.

Figure 1 illustrates the argument.

The illustration is self-explanatory. We only need to add that the net outflow of exploited capital (and other values) from the periphery is the net result of all the imperialist processes. This should not be surprising. After all, this is a capitalist world. It may come with other net costs to the periphery, such as costs in the weakening of internal-periphery economic conditions, political subordination of the periphery, violent de-culturalization and enculturalization, and so on, but all these are means, or accompanying undertones, to the capitalist historic theme of accumulating capital in the centre at the expense of the periphery.

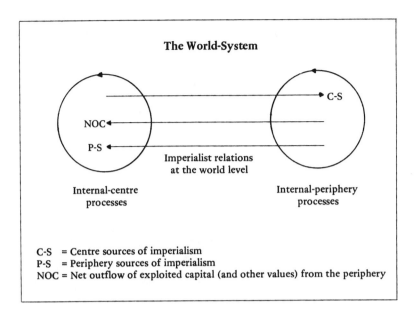

FIG. 1. Net capital flow in the world-system

How does this simple sketch illustrate the continuity of imperialism thesis throughout capitalist history?

Simplifying the above sketch a little and recalling the correspondence between phases of world capitalism and phases of imperialism established in chapter six, it may become easy to appreciate that the continuity resides precisely in the continuous net outflow of capital and other valuables from the periphery to the centre all through the history of capitalism, changes in the processes in the centre, in the periphery, and in the relations between the two notwithstanding. What follows in figure 2 relates net outflow of capital and other valuables (P → C), the phases of world capitalism (1−6), and the main phases of world imperialism (1−6).

The Thesis and Some Clarifications

This scheme may raise many questions, but there is a question that must be raised now, because we cannot, nor should we, seek to hide it. It is this: If we base our reasoning on imperialism essentially on the continuity of the relations and the interactions between its internal-centre and its

135

World-Capitalist Phases	Corresponding Main Imperialist Phases
1. Early mercantilist, 1500–1640s	1. C ○──────○ P Plunder, settlements, and incursions
2. Mercantilist, 1640s–1750s	2. C ○──────○ P 1 + trade
3. Classical capitalism, 1750s–1870s	3. C ○──────○ P 1 - 2 + accelerated colonialism and firm footing dependency
4. Monopoly capitalism, 1870s–1950s	4. C ○──────○ P 1 - 3 + maturing of dependency and neo-colonialism
5. TNC and NIDL capitalism, 1950–present	5. C ○──────○ P Dependency and neo-colonialism mature into demands for NIEO
6. Post-NIDL, present(?)–?	6. C ○──────○ P P = periphery C = centre

FIG. 2. The correspondence between capitalism and imperialism

internal-periphery sources, resulting in the outflow of capital from the periphery, that is, if we suggest peripheral participation in imperialism from the very beginning, how do we explain the absence of "capital" in the periphery at the earliest phase and the absence of internal periphery sources of imperialism at this phase in world-history?

As to the absence of capital in the periphery in the first phase of imperialism, all we can say is that this is one of the good examples of Eurocentric magical designation of categories. Capital was given the categorical meaning of being something which was produced under certain given conditions which were said to be present only in Europe at a particular time. Anything else resembling capital, or claiming to be capital, is conveniently consigned to the less illustrious realms of pre-capital and prehistory of capital. This way of viewing capital focuses the history of the world on Europe and European variables and constancies excessively to the unacceptable neglect of other variables and constancies which are important for understanding world-history.

Within European history alone, the pre-capital/capital distinction is perhaps not offensive. In the context of world-history, however, the prominence of capital is so great that we should be careful not to overdraw the difference between its so-called prehistory and history forms. For, if we overdraw this distinction, we ignore a large part of the early contributions of the non-European parts of the world to the formation and the meaning of world-history. Whatever was taken from the natives and societies of Latin America, North America, Asia, and Africa before capital matured in Europe, from the world-system perspective, is barely distinguishable from capital itself. Therefore, from our perspective, I choose to place emphasis on the functional *similarities* between *pre-capital* and *capital* rather than the *differences* between them: the earlier world-involved history and processes of accumulating capital in Europe prior to the nineteenth century are part of the total history of accumulating capital within the capitalist historicity. From the world-system historiographic point of view, these earlier processes of accumulating capital, at the very least, rank in all respects with capital as an already accumulated thing.

The first contacts between the initial European "expanders" and societies of the periphery were always established by brute force and/or the betrayal of the trust of these societies in professed European intentions. Where local conditions allowed plundering to proceed unhindered — and there must have been only a few such cases, if any at all — plundering must have proceeded with latent, even if "unintended," interference in local situations. But where such initial brutal contacts were resisted — and this must have been in most cases — the European expanders must have exploited local rivalries to gain footholds in local situations after which they must have set about constructing the bridgeheads for smooth plundering and further expansion. These initial processes are those that inserted world-history in the many local histories in the periphery and thereby brought these histories into world-history.

What is significant in this regard is not how long or short the individual initial insertions took. What is significant is precisely that the very processes of initial insertions meant more than European interference in the different local histories; they meant the simultaneous creation by many different means (raw white settlements, machiavellian involvement in local situations, alliances, outright conquest, etc.) of internal-periphery imperialist sources. The nature of these initial sources must have differed. Some must have centred on local chiefs and kings, some on rebellious sections in some societies, and some on weak national groups. Some of these sources must have been strong, some weak. Some must have lasted and, yet, some must have broken down, calling for the entire process to start all over again.

Neither of these things is more significant, however, than the fact that no matter how insecure, how uncertain, how unsuspecting, and how resistant these initial sources were, they all developed effective sources of and mechanisms for capital leaks from the periphery to the centre.

A study of the right column of figure 2 will indicate how, from their uncertain and insecure origins, the sources have grown progressively in competence, stature, and in confidence to the point where they now come in the sophisticated forms of neo-colonialist sovereign states clamouring for both the recognition and the intensification of the dependent insertions of their economies and societies into the world-system, through their insistent demands for a New International Economic Order (NIEO).

As figure 2 indicates, just when world capitalism assumed the transnational corporation (TNC) and the New International Division of Labour (NIDL) combination form, just when capital had become truly world-wide, the reality of the continuity of imperialism made it possible for neo-colonialism to become strong enough to demand the NIEO, so that capital can be guaranteed to desert the periphery in more subtle and more efficient ways.

But what is the TNC-NIDL combination, what does it mean; and what is the NIEO? And in which way does the postulated correspondence between them clarify the *thesis*?

Transnational corporations are the "new" forms of dominant capital and capital-producing forms. These forms have outgrown the traditional capital home boundaries of nation-states and have come to assume a world-wide character and a mobility of their own. For the TNCs, the world is now the *home*. Nation-states are merely their respective *houses*.[16]

The New International Divison of Labour defies a brief presentation. Essentially, it is a new phase in the development of world capitalism, its latest and current phase. It refers to a new set of preconditions which capital itself, through its long history, has created to facilitate its own efficient expansion. It is the latest dominant expression of the conscious and the deliberate method of accumulating capital in the ever-changing circumstances in the evolution of world capitalism.

According to a group of researchers, who were among the first to detect the NIDL, this new phase of capitalism was ushered in by the crisis in the world-economy in the mid-1970s.[17] The characteristics of this crisis may be many, but this group of researchers suggests that they include the following: consistently high unemployment rates in the traditional industrial countries; cut-backs in production, over-capacity, "short-time" labour, and mass dismissals in an increasing number of industrial branches of the traditional industrial countries; a leap forward in the rationalization and automatization of the production process brought about by the shift from electro-mechanical to electronic components; an often stagnant or even declining rate of investment in the industrial countries; a prevalence of rationalization schemes rather than of investment in the replacement of capital equipment and in the expansion of production within the traditional industrial countries; increasing occupational "mobility" forced upon skilled labour; the fiscal crisis of the state due to an increase in social expenditure; encouragement by the state for private business to invest domestically through the provision of increasingly higher state financial inputs into private business; the proletarianization and impoverishment of ever-growing numbers of people in the underdeveloped countries; the establishment of a world-oriented manufacturing industry in many underdeveloped countries, characterized by a fragmented production process, and constituting a dependent form of "blocked" or mono-industrialization; and, finally, the increasing interpenetration of national economies today.[18]

The crisis may have brought about the NIDL, but the crisis is not the NIDL. The emergence of the NIDL from the crisis is a demonstration of world capitalism's ingenuity for adaptation and a testimony to its resilience and durability.

The authors argue that the nature of the crisis has brought about a dislocation in "the old or classical division of labour, where the underdeveloped countries were on the whole only incorporated into the capitalist world-economy as raw-material suppliers, [which] no longer exists today."[19] In its place, is what they describe as the NIDL.

Essentially, the NIDL has been brought about by three developments. They are:
— "the development of a world-wide 'reservoir' of potential labour force ... practically inexhaustible ... in Asia, Africa, and Latin America";[20]
— "the development of a technology which renders industrial location and the direction of production itself less dependent on geographical distances";[21]
— "the development and refinement of technology and labour organization which makes it possible to decompose complex production processes into elementary units so that even an unskilled labour force can easily and quickly be trained to perform otherwise complex operations (fragmentation of jobs)."[22]

As the authors argue, it is "the coincidence of [these three developments, and their many constituent factors, which] has created a qualitatively new set of preconditions for the expansion and accumulation of capital. It has given a further impetus to the development of an international capital market ... and, more generally, to the development of elements of an international superstructure."[23] The authors remind us that "certain *elements* of these preconditions were ... already shaped in one form or another at a much earlier period — at least in the beginning, not necessarily under the direct and conscious control of capital."[24]

But this is not the argument. The argument is that now the elements of the preconditions are developed enough and are realized as such by capital for them to constitute a clear departure from the old international division of labour.

What is in this departure for the periphery of the world-economy? This question is very important; and I shall use its importance and the clarity of the authors' position to justify the need for the following long quote concerning their main thesis:

The main thesis, now, is that this complete, qualitatively new set of preconditions for the expansion and accumulation of capital has only emerged in the 1960s. A single world market for labour and a single world market in industrial sites now, for the first time, effectively emcompasses both the traditional industrial countries as well as the underdeveloped countries. In many cases, industrial capital, confronted with this set of preconditions, can earn extra profits through a suitable reorganization of production, because a suitable subdivision of the production process makes it possible to exploit the *world-wide* industrial reserve army with the help of a highly developed transport and communication system. Under the force of competition, the individual capital is compelled in these cases to relocate abroad to ensure the expansion of capital. This often means that, for the first time in the history of the capitalist world economy, sites for the production of semi-processed and processed manufactured goods are located in the underdeveloped countries on a profitable as well as world-wide competitive basis. Goods are largely produced for export since internal demand is extremely weak in these countries (a condition brought about by the development of the capitalist world economy itself).

This tendency which (a) is bound to break up the traditional bisection of the world into a few industrial countries on the one hand, the great majority of developing countries incorporated into the capitalist world economy only as raw-material suppliers, on the other, and (b) which enforces increasing subdivision of the manufacturing processes into separate partial productions in different locations around the world, will be designated by the term "the new international division of labour" (a division of labour which is to be considered as an on-going process and not as a completed state). This new international division of labour is, then, an "institutional" innovation of capital itself (enforced by the new preconditions expansion and accumulation of capital), and not at all the result of changed development strategies of individual countries or of fortuitous decisions of so-called multinational companies. The fact that individual countries and companies today are forced to adjust their policies in respect to an expansive strategy of capital under changed conditions (read: requirements brought about by the world market in industrial sites), is a manifestation of a qualitative transformation in the preconditions for the expansion and accumulation of capital.

To pose the problem in terms of an absolute fall in the profit rate in the traditional industrial countries which, in turn, forces capital to relocate parts of its production, would be quite inadequate judged from the approach taken here. It is not our purpose here to dispute the possible existence of such a fall in the profit rate. The question to be answered (which is, in fact, already answered by the world-wide movements of capital) is simply *whether* it is production at the traditional sites or production at new sites that provides for a better expansion and accumulation of capital under "given" conditions (or, more precisely, for expansion and accumulation at all). (Emphases added.)[25]

Indeed, the question is *whether*. And, as can be seen, there is not much in this new development which works for the autonomous and non-dependent, even if related, generation and accumulation of capital in the peripheral societies. The plausibility of our *thesis* is further strengthened when we realize that, as it was in the very beginning, when Europe used the non-European parts of the world to solve the European feudal crisis, so it is today that world capital, housed in Europe, uses the non-European societies and states to solve a crisis which in its origins, in the 1960s and 1970s, was particularly European. The result is the same. Capital continues to desert the periphery for the centre. Nothing has changed, then, in the nature of imperialism, even if its forms, the modes of generating exploitation of the periphery, have changed. Can, and will, the NIEO help the situation? A fuller treatment of this question has been done elsewhere; and the verdict seems to be that the NIEO cannot.[26]

The NIEO corresponds to the NIDL phase of world capitalism as much as the earliest internal-periphery sources of imperialism corresponded to the early mercantilist phase of world-history. Referring to figure 2, I shall argue that the plausibility of our thesis is sustained by the *continuity* logic in what we have been discussing in this section, as much as anything else, and that it is confidently illustrated by the arrows P_1C_1 to P_6C_6 and by C_1C_6 in the right column of figure 2.

At this point, let us recall Amin. His position, to the effect that primitive accumulation is permanent and contemporary, is theoretically sustained from our perspective: primitive accumulation in Europe from the periphery is *continuous* all through world-history and, therefore, *permanent* in this history.

I shall say, then, that in the history of capital, what should be clear is that it develops capitalism, "warts and all," in the centre,[27] and develops in the periphery *all the warts without capitalism.* What exists in the periphery is, as Amin puts it, *peripheral capitalism*, with all its historic inability to accumulate capital because of its very participation in the capitalist world-economy. This is a historical legacy of the capitalist world and an essential part of the conceptual and the theoretical definitions of the world-system's capitalist historicity.

The Thesis and Some Derivative Hypotheses

Some hypotheses can be derived from our *thesis*, as presented above, without too much effort.

The *first hypothesis* is that, from what we have been discussing so far, it should be pretty clear that, from this point in time and looking on history, imperialism, as a process, a relational phenomenon, appears to be a curious social matter in which the roles of the participants — the victims and the culprits — appear to become more and more (extended and) reinforced as the process continues. It is true that the process itself will negate itself some day. But is it also not clear that this hypothesis tells us that, to negate it soon enough, we should take a good critical look at the reasons for its long continuity so that we can derive the philosophy of our praxis from its true history, its continuity?

The *second hypothesis* which can be derived immediately from the *thesis* is that, for as long as the world-system, that is essentially the world-economy, remains capitalist beyond the present (stage 6 in fig. 2), capital and other valuables will continue to desert the periphery.

The *third hypothesis* which can be derived is that, for as long as development has something to do with the generation and the retention of capital within national boundaries and/or with the generation of capital in the world and its equal accumulated and accumulating incidence all over the world for the purpose of enhancing human dignity, the periphery cannot develop as much as it otherwise could, Eurocentric appearances to the contrary notwithstanding.

This leads to a *fourth hypothesis*. It is that, even in the event of the present world capitalist formation yielding to a "socialist" order but an order which pursues the accumulation of capital in the fashion of the present "socialist" orders, the periphery still cannot develop to the extent that it could. This is because, given the nature and the nascence of any such "socialist" order, as we can understand it today, such an order will still be Eurocentric and capital will still desert the periphery for the centre, because, by all appearances, such an order will continue to be Eurocentrically *developmentalist* and *developmental*.[28]

A *fifth hypothesis*, which is in fact a thesis in its own right but which we cannot avoid confronting in this context, is whether, given the four hypotheses deriving from the *thesis*, the very idea of *development* itself, from the periphery's perspective, should not come to mean the negation of capitalist exploitation understood to mean the negation of both internal-periphery and world-system-level capitalist exploitations. This is important because, as we can glean from the above, internal-periphery capitalist exploitation is not only directly related to world-system imperialist exploitation but is a critical, integral part of it. This will mean that we cannot hope to negate one type of exploitation without negating the other type.

Notes

1. See chapter three.
2. See chapters four and five.
3. Jonathan Friedman, "Crises in the Theory of Transformations of the World Economy," *Review* 2, no. 2 (1978): 131–146.
4. Friedman (see note 3 above), p. 135.
5. Friedman (see note 3 above), p. 135.
6. Friedman (see note 3 above), p. 135.
7. Friedman (see note 3 above), pp. 135–136.
8. Friedman (see note 3 above), p. 136.
9. Friedman (see note 3 above), p. 136.
10. Friedman (see note 3 above), p. 136.
11. Bill Warren, "Imperialism and Capitalist Industrialization," *New Left Review* 81 (Sept.–Oct. 1973): 3–44; and also his *Imperialism, The Pioneer of Capitalism* (NLB, London, 1980). Recall G. Palma, "Dependency: A Formal Theory of Underdevelopment or a Methodology for the Analysis of Concrete Situations of Underdevelopment?" *World Development* 6:881–924. See also Fernando H. Cardoso and Enzo Faletto, *Dependency and Development in Latin America* (University of California Press, Berkeley, Cal., 1979).
12. J. Galtung, "Global Goals, Global Processes and the Prospects for Human and Social Development" (Mimeo, 1979), p. 14.
13. Some students of the subject think that these interrelationships need not be complex. One of them is Ian Roxborough, *Theories of Underdevelopment* (Macmillan, London, 1979).

14. We need to be sensitized to the distinction between *real* and *apparent* change. See Roy Prieswerk, "Hidden Dimensions of the So-Called New International Economic Order," in Herb Addo, ed., *Transforming the World-Economy? Nine Critical Essays on the New International Economic Order* (Hodder and Stoughton, London, 1984).

15. B. Sutcliffe, "Conclusion," in R. Owen and B. Sutcliffe, eds., *Studies in the Theory of Imperialism* (Longman, London, 1972).

16. There are many works on TNCs. But Stephen Hymer's essays on the subject still remain some of the most penetrating. See, among other works, Robert B. Cohen et al., eds., *The Multinational Corporation: A Radical Approach, Papers by Stephen Herbert Hymer* (Cambridge University Press, London, 1979).

17. They are Folker Fröbel, Jürgen Heinrichs, and Otto Kreye, formerly of the Max-Planck-Institut zur Erforschung der Lebensbedingungen der wissenschaftlich-technischen Welt, Starnberg, FRG. Because of the masterful clarity of their arguments to describe and explain the current world-economic situation, I rely heavily on their "The New International Division of Labour," *Social Science Information* 17, no. 1 (1978): 123–142, and their "The Tendency Towards a New International Division of Labour," *Review* 1, no. 1 (1977): 73–88. For further theoretical aspects to the subject and their empirical validations, see their *The New International Division of Labour* (Cambridge University Press, London, 1980).

18. Taken from Fröbel et al., "The New International Division of Labour" (see note 17 above), p. 124. On the matter of crisis, see Andre Gunder Frank, *Crisis: In the Third World* (Holmes and Meier, New York, 1980); *Crisis: In the World Economy* (Holmes and Meier, New York, 1980); and his "World Crisis, Theory and Ideology," a paper presented at the colloquium on "Nationalism and Capitalism in Crisis," Max-Planck-Institut, Starnberg, 25–27 June 1980. See also Immanuel Wallerstein, "Nationalism and the World Transition to Socialism: Is There a Crisis?" a paper presented at the above colloquium; Folker Fröbel, "The Current Development of the World Economy (Research paper, United Nations University, Tokyo, 1980); and Otto Kreye, "Perspectives for Development through Industrialization in the 1980s: An Independent Viewpoint on Dependency" (Research paper, United Nations University, Tokyo, 1980).

19. Fröbel et al., "The New International Division of Labour" (see note 17 above), p. 125.

20. Fröbel et al., "The New International Division of Labour" (see note 17 above), p. 126.

21. Fröbel et al., "The New International Division of Labour" (see note 17 above), p. 127.

22. Fröbel et al., "The New International Division of Labour" (see note 17 above), p. 128.

23. Fröbel et al., "The New International Division of Labour" (see note 17 above), p. 129.

24. Fröbel et al., "The New International Division of Labour" (see note 17 above), p. 129.

25. Fröbel et al., "The New International Division of Labour" (see note 17 above), pp. 130–131. See also Fröbel et al., "The Tendency Towards a New International Division of Labour" (note 17 above), p. 83.

26. See Herb Addo, ed., *Transforming the World-Economy?* (note 14 above).

27. See the reference to Palma at the end of chapter six.

28. For a fuller discussion, see Herb Addo et al., *Development as Social Transformation: Reflections on the Global Problematique* (Hodder and Stoughton, London, 1985).

Part Four

Challenges and Responses

Chapter Eight

Questions and Answers

Pressure to Deepen the Thesis

Patrick Healey: I would like you to clarify what it is that you mean by Eurocentricity. Does this mean merely that theories start and deal with "Europe," or more? Are the concepts Eurocentric in some deeper sense? If this latter, what is the deeper sense, and what would an alternative look like? Possible alternatives could be:
— fill in missing bits from a periphery view;
— scrap the terms "centre" and "periphery" and change the entire perspective; or
— assert the prehistory of the periphery.

Would I be right in saying that what you are suggesting in fact by your Eurocentric indictment is that we should not mix old ingredients to explain old Eurocentric problematics, but that we should mix new conceptual ingredients in such ways as will provide a qualitatively new approach to the understanding of the world. If this, what would it be, what would be the characteristics, etc., of this new mixture, bearing in mind that in your scheme, in order to understand the world in the last 500 years or so, expansion from Europe, capitalism, and imperialism are *vital*?

Herb Addo: I am glad to clarify for you, the best I can, what it is that I mean by Eurocentricity. Essentially, what I mean is that were an extra-terrestial creature to suddenly appear on earth and were this creature to be confronted with the historiographic and epistemological bases of political economy, he could be pardoned if he were to conclude that the heroics and the poetics of world-history are all totally European. It would be difficult for him to appreciate that other parts of the world played any roles in the development of our world capitalist civilization.

This is because in "some deeper sense," yet to be fully articulated, the developmentalist philosophy of the modern world-system is European-centred; and this is because in "some deeper sense" the basis of what is considered valid knowledge is European-dictated. It is when we put these two things together that I think we begin to approach the deeper or inner meaning of Eurocentricity.

What is involved calls for much more than "filling in missing bits from a periphery view," even though this would be as good a starting point as any.

It does not call for the scrapping of the terms "centre" and "periphery." Rather it calls for the recognition of the dialectical unity between these two historical concepts and the recognition of the dominance relation between them. The "entire perspective," as you put it, would have changed once we learn to confront centre-domination, with its dialectical periphery-subordination, in seeking to find out why both have become *what they are* instead of *what they could have been*, with a keen eye on what they should preferably be in the transformed future.[1]

In all this, the "prehistories" of all societies matter for transformational valuation purposes; but we cannot do this to any meaningful extent if we do not challenge Eurocentric precepts and theories, indeed their epistemological foundations. It is suggested that out of this challenge may come what may well be what you describe as a "qualitatively new approach to the understanding of the world." All this is without prejudice to European dominance in world-history. In fact, it calls for its vital recognition as the first step.

Johan Galtung: My first question is along the lines indicated by Patrick Healey. I shall approach it as Lincoln approached his definition of democracy at Gettysburg. What does Eurocentrism mean to you? From what you are saying, there are four possible interpretations:
1. Eurocentricism *of* European action, tied to concrete European history;
2. Eurocentricism *by* Europeans, that is, written by Europeans, some of them in non-white skins.

Addo: Very true! In all kinds of skins.

Galtung: Let me finish, please.
3. Eurocentricism *for* Europeans, that is, for analysing that which means

something, positive or negative, for Europe and Europeans; or
4. that we have become used to thinking about imperialism in such a way
that our conceptual net captures certain things rather than others. And
here I refer you to Miklos Molnar's work on Marxism and
international relations.[2]
If the latter, I would like to see the deeper sense of the term spelt out and
also I would like you to indicate *why* and *how* one could develop
alternative conceptual networks.

Addo: Could you expand a bit more, Johan, on the last part of your
question — the part dealing with the *why* and *how* one can develop
alternative conceptual networks?

Galtung: All right, I shall. What I mean is that an answer could be that:
there exist also *other* imperialisms, *by* others, to distribute better the
whole enterprise of analysing imperialism; so that one sees better what it
means to *others*, such as the dependencia theorists, and Walter Rodney,
as in his *How Europe Underdeveloped Africa*, for example. And there is
the world-system approach; but this approach is also suffering from the
fallacy of Marxism in the Wallerstein version, which is no more than a
book-keeping, accountant, approach, showing that somebody was
short-sighted and somebody was not. But then, there are also other
approaches dealing with how other aspects of human beings are touched
and understand the touch, cosmology, for example.

What would you pick out of all that?

Addo: Now that I understand you, I will take all that and respond to it in
some detail.

With respect to the Lincolnian parallel, I think my view of the matter is
well captured by your reference to the *of, by,* and *for* Europe(ans). Thank
you for the reference to Molnar's work. And since you have done me this
favour, let me return the favour. Let me refer you to your own two
volumes on *Methodology and Ideology*.[3] Incidentally, I think those two
volumes are mistitled. I think they should have been called "Methodology
as Ideology." You argue persuasively there that there is no
methodology/epistemology without an attendant ideology. I agree with
you wholly. All I am saying, then, is that the ethos of the dominant
ideology is Eurocentric. I use my treatment of imperialism to suggest
that, among others, your own position has (some) validity.

I would like to think that the way I have handled the argument must suggest, at the very least, that "our conceptual net captures certain things and not others." The treatment of imperialism here is only meant to point to the highly probable validity of the Eurocentric charge and no more. It is beyond me at the moment to demonstrate this validity beyond *all* doubt, reasonable and otherwise.

The demand to provide a *deeper* sense of the Eurocentric indictment may be a reasonable one. For obvious reasons, I need time to formulate such a meaning, if it is at all possible.

On *other* imperialisms, yes, I agree with you, if you put it that way. There are other forms of exploitation that are themselves used by capitalist exploitation to drain capital and valuables from the periphery. To use a term Kimon Valaskakis has used a lot, capitalist imperialism has always "piggy-backed" on other forms of exploitation which are conducive to the draining of capital from the periphery.

With such a viewpoint, we are in a better position to approach the dependencia theorists and the Rodney thesis of how Europe underdeveloped Africa, by asking whether Europe alone *was* and *continues* to be responsible for the underdevelopment of Africa and other parts of the periphery. This, frankly, is the larger question I am primarily interested in, as some of the draft chapters may indicate and for which the present endeavour is no more than a very long introduction.

Other approaches, for example, the cosmology/eschatology mode of explanation, are no less valid. My present feeling is that my approach to the subject does not exclude them.

Lastly, it may well be that the world-system approach is exactly how you describe it, "a book-keeping, accountant, approach." But I believe that it is the kind of "accountant" approach that will lead to further investigation that, in turn, will lead to the discovery of a multi-million-dollar Eurocentric epistemological fraud.

Neville Duncan: My intervention deals with what appears to me to be your main plank in the Eurocentric indictment, which deals with the point that to Eurocentrics the world appears to matter only because Europe is in it. My argument is this: Europe matters not merely because it is part of the world, but, because of a certain set of factors, it managed to go further ahead, in special (Eurocentric?) directions, of other countries and somehow has found other ways to continue to maintain the reality and the illusion of dominance in the face of the US extension to, and the Japanese challenge for, inclusion in this reality and illusion.

The notion for this query came from Wallerstein, *The Modern World-System*,[4] where he argued that Europe itself had created nothing, it merely synthesized development in China, Africa, and Asia in directions in which the former areas' value preferences and cultures did not permit them.

Perhaps Weber was right to think that he could do a Marx with the role of ideas in capitalism (the Eurocentric version, of course) and evaluate the capitalist ethic.

Addo: You are referring to the Protestant ethic and all that.[5]

Duncan: Yes, and all that.

Referring to your earlier point dealing with history as the pursuit (advance and retreat) of social values, this is perhaps another reason why you need a *histroid*,[6] why China needed and needs a cultural revolution, why the Islamic world is so resistant and "perverse," and why Castro needed to create the new "socialist man."

Addo: You forgot to add Kwame Nkrumah's new "African man." He gave the portrait of such a man once in a speech. I heard him, on the radio.[7]

I agree with you totally. Any misconception in this regard is my own. I should have made it very clear at the start what it was that I meant by Europe. The United States is part of Europe of the Diaspora.[8]

Europe, larger Europe, may not have created anything, but it did use others and other things to dominate the modern world. This is what I find fascinating. Weber tried; and others have tried, too. The question is: What are the other systems of ethics and how can they aid the transformation of the world? This is where perhaps cosmology comes in; but to me these other ethics are to be studied not for themselves but in terms of what their various encounters in world-history have made of them with reference to the transformational potential inherent in our current system.

Again, I agree with you that we need a *histroid*; but then again, this becomes interesting to me only if we relate all this to the persistence of capitalism, especially the persistence of its peripheral subpart.

Healey: I would think you still need a chapter to clarify what it is that you mean and call Eurocentricity, if it includes all that.

Addo: I am beginning to think that I need to do more than add a chapter to clarify what I mean. I need to deepen the meaning of Eurocentricity. To do this properly, a chapter, no matter how long, clear, and detailed, will not be enough. To do this well, I need a lot of speculative space. A second volume is what I am beginning to think I need, if I am to do the subject full justice.

George Aseniero: Listening to you over the last couple of days, one question is inescapable. It is this: What will happen if the *historic theme* is to change; and how will this change relate to imperialism?

Addo: I am glad for this question in that it affords me the opportunity to say that the historic interpretation of capitalism is only introduced here without the full elaboration it deserves. I intended to do this at a later date, but as the idea of the second volume takes hold in my mind, I begin to think it should be done there, perhaps.

However, to answer your question, I will say that once the historic theme remains the same, that is, for as long as there is the accumulation of capital on a world scale and the leakage of generated capital from the periphery, nothing happens to imperialism, it remains, it persists. But once the historic theme changes, the other historic properties, including imperialism, change, too.

It is not easy to say what they will change into, but the essential point is that the change in the historic theme must be total, transformational, not partial, as we have in the various socialist revolutions, where transitional impulses and tendencies are frozen into unfinished social projects and glibly pronounced accomplished revolutionary transformations. If the change in the historic theme is not total, other historic properties, including imperialism, will persist in barely disguised forms. The Soviet invasion of Afghanistan, for example, is as imperialist as any in the history of capitalism.

Helen McEachrane: My current interest is in the New International Economic Order (the NIEO) and I know that it is also one of your current interests. I shall therefore ask you this question: To the extent that the NIEO is Eurocentric, what other kinds of ingredients, do you think, would be needed for the NIEO to be de-Eurocentricized?

Addo: A lot of ingredients. I know it is superfluous for me to refer you to our volume on the NIEO,[9] but, as you know, in that volume we try to point to some of the ingredients. Specifically, the chapters by Roy Prieswerk, Andre Gunder Frank, and George Aseniero, address themselves directly to this question. For my part, I will say that the main ingredient is the need to de-Eurocentricize what development is supposed to mean.[10] But I argue that this cannot be done without the de-Eurocentricization (a clumsy term, I admit) of the dominant developmentalist epistemology.

Insofar as I know and understand the contents of the NIEO demands, the motive behind them, and the politics of their pursuit, there is not much that can be said to be *really* new in the package of demands called the NIEO.

A look at the package reveals it to be only a little more than a collection of all the old developmental slogans that have been making the international rounds since the end of the Second World War.[11]

The truth appears to be that, as each slogan proved developmentally worthless, even damaging, they were all put together in the early to mid-1970s and presented with all the colourful flamboyance at the command of our contemporary malady of the "mythology of change." As a *goal*, a *tactic*, or a wholesome *strategy*, the NIEO is transformationally uncertain, even perhaps worthless. As a philosophy for the transformation of the world-economy, and the world-system, it is embarrassing, for the motive behind the demands for the NIEO appear to be, sadly, not merely the blind imitation of the Eurocentric "bourgeois way of life" by the élites in the periphery, but, more seriously, a determined craving for it. I cannot think of anything that will give a longer lease of life to imperialism than this.

The politics for pursuing the actualization of a NIEO are not informed by a proper reading of the history of the subordination of the periphery by the centre in world-history. What is even pathetic in all this is that the intention behind the NIEO is not informed by the necessity to actualize internally in peripheral societies exactly the same just and equitable order that these states claim they seek at the international level.

The NIEO is not a transformational device. It is a plea for further penetration into the economies and the societies of the periphery; and it amounts to a demand for the formal integration of their élites into the international system of élites.

McEachrane: Where does class conflict come in here and other aspects of your thoughts?

Addo: Very much part of what I will call the necessary transformational "tool kit." But I doubt very much whether, in all circumstances, it is the tool of the most consequence. I say this, knowing full well that it is not a popular view to express.

Galtung: Let me add to all that, then, to round off the inquiry into the NIEO.

Is the point that development is *not* a fight against capitalism and imperialism? For if they are Eurocentrically conceived, then development definition and concepts will only be reactive and imitative: *reactive* by defence, beating Western imperialism as that has been defined by the enemy; *imitative* by trying to get for oneself the same as Europe got through imperialism and other exploitative mechanisms at home and abroad.

Addo: Yes, I agree with you entirely. This is a basic matter of grave transformation concern: the very idea of development has to be newly conceived. It has to be de-Eurocentricized, totally. This is what some of us have been trying to do within the GPID and elsewhere.[12]

Galtung: Is one of the major defences, perhaps the only viable defence, not the institution of egalitarian systems in third world societies?

Addo: Yes, I could not agree more. I share this view and I adopt it in my NIEO chapter.

Pressure to Widen the Thesis

Kimon Valaskakis: I would like to ask you some questions I consider fundamental to the clarification of your Eurocentric thesis. I have two questions.

First, do you challenge Eurocentricity as a *fact* of life, or do you *recognize* it as a fact of life and therefore you argue that in the future it is desirable this no longer be so. On this matter, I will argue that Eurocentricity is a fact of life because: (1) the European lifestyle predominates; and (2) even critics of Eurocentricity are usually European or Euro-trained.

Addo: On your first question my response will be that I *recognize* Eurocentricity as an unpleasant fact of life but I *challenge* its claim to universal validity. I regard it as an invalid fact of life, if you prefer that formulation, because it is an all-round inhibiting fact of life. The *predominance* of European life does not necessarily make it valid. And you are right in saying that even critics of Eurocentricity are usually European or Euro-trained. But then, how else can it be? It must take a disenchanted Eurocentric to point out the invalidity of Eurocentricity.

Permit me to refer to my notes anticipating this fundamental criticism. I note here that the only way out of this bind is to admit that I was, for a long time, a Euro-trained and an uncompromising Eurocentric; and that now I am a disenchanted Eurocentric.[13] My critique of Eurocentricity is to be understood in this light: It will always take a disenchanted witch to point out a witch, as a Ghanaian proverb says.

Valaskakis: My second question deals with the relationship between capitalism and imperialism. In this regard, I request clarification on your Eurocentricity thesis, as I can read into this thesis four competing interpretations: (1) capitalism means a form of imperialism; (2) imperialism means a form of capitalism; (3) both are similar in some vital respects; and (4) the two are identical.

Addo: Thanks for your second question. It enables me to clarify a point. Capitalism does not mean a form of imperialism; neither does imperialism mean a form of capitalism. Capitalism breeds a particular form of exploitation as its abiding attribute. The *particularity* of this form of exploitation resides in the increasing *efficiency* of its operation. I do not see capitalism and imperialism as merely similar in vital respects, I see them as synonymous, you may prefer identical, precisely because to me the effects of both on third world societies are the same: efficient exploitation and effective subjugation of these societies.

Valaskakis: Well, let me be clear.

Addo: By all means.

Valaskakis: If identical, then are you not engaged in a phoney semantic battle? What will you call Roman exploitation? Imperialism or what? Are you talking about a family of exploitative relations and mechanisms, a member of which is Roman imperialism, another of which is the Soviet invasion of Afghanistan? In deciding which is which, I must remind you to avoid tempo-centrism, as capitalism is but a footnote in history; and you must not forget that even within capitalism there were/are phases of imperialism, mercantilism, the nineteenth century wave, and the form of imperialism which is purely economic.

Addo: Far from it. I do not think that I am at all involved in a phoney semantic battle. I have given a lot of thought to this matter. I am pleading for a *precise* analytic use of a key historical concept. In a very *imprecise* way and at the first encounter, yes, I am referring to a family of exploitative relations and mechanisms, a sempiternal agony in human history. But my argument is that such a reference is of no great historico-analytical use. If we are going to be historically specific, then we will have to acknowledge that Roman exploitation and Soviet exploitation belong to different historic periods and, therefore, what is interesting is not their outward similarities, but rather their inner differences.

The Roman and the current forms differ in their efficiencies and even in some of the mechanisms employed. This is important. We should not ignore it. If we are going to be historically specific, and therefore precise, we must realize that the forms in question belong to different historic epochs. I try to avoid tempo-centrism. That is exactly what I criticize the orthodox Marxists for. I disagree that capitalism is but a footnote in history — in all human history, perhaps, but then that is exactly what I criticize the liberals for.

I agree that there were/are phases of imperialism, but I disagree that there is anything like purely economic imperialism unto itself. The economic, cultural, political, and other aspects of imperialism are all so intimately part of the exploitative reality that to separate them is a dangerous business. It can lead to all sorts of alibis, such as that the US involvement in Viet Nam was not economic imperialism but political or strategic, or that the Soviet invasion of Afghanistan is pre-emptive strategic. This is dangerous; it defines the concept's historic meaning and identity away for no good reason.

Duncan: I would like you to relate your expositions of imperialism and capitalism to each other, through the mediation of your exposition on exploitation. The question, then, is this: How do you link the exploitation of imperialism with the exploitation of capitalism (I assume they are different and operate on different groups/classes of people in different locations in the "definite system of production") as a way of challenging the capitalist/imperialist domination of the content of what you term in your presentation on capitalism as the *historic force* of the efficiency of exploitation of both human and non-human resources, the *historic theme* of capital accumulation, and the *historic motive* of the pursuit of the bourgeois way of life and the proletarian way of life.

What I am interested in hearing you express yourself on is this: *How* is one to begin the process of formulating a feasible and desirable alternative to the existing world/national order?

Allow me, in this context, to allude to Andre Gorz's work, where he argues that a commonality of interest in destroying the world order is present between certain exploited classes in the centre as well as the periphery.[14] The problem would be how could they see eye to eye and organize formally and ideologically on a basis which would challenge imperialism/capitalism successfully?

Finally, and in relation to an earlier intervention,[15] where do race and ethnicity fit in your conception of imperialism? Do they have any relevance at all?

Addo: The relationship between the two, capitalism and imperialism, and their conjoint mediation through exploitation is intriguing, even if problematic. I have a few initial thoughts on this matter, as you know.[16] You are asking, and rightly so, for the further development of the thoughts. I wonder very much if I can improve on this in a hurry. I need time. The same goes for the historic conception of history and its application to capitalist history, world-history.[17]

I rather prefer not to talk too much about it till I have had time to reflect on it much better. As this discussion progresses, I begin to be convinced of the need to divide the manuscript into two volumes: one establishing the continuity of imperialism thesis and the other deepening the

Eurocentric critique and relating it to elaborate treatment of the historic conception of capitalism, development, race ethnicity, etc.

I shall stop short, then, in responding to your query on worker commonality of interest in detail, except to say that it appears to me that the primacy of class and international worker solidarity is Eurocentrically imposed. On this matter I shall argue that the objective commonality of interest exists, but it is obscured by Eurocentricity. It obscures the formal and the ideological organization of it. I am very much of the opinion that it is a nice formula but an awful reality. Having read Bettleheim's self-incriminating critique of Emmanuel,[18] I am inclined to believe that this nice formula may well be a Eurocentric device, part of its methodological armoury.[19]

Thank you for your reference to Gorz's work. We need to see Eurocentricity for what it is before we can start worrying about how we can make all workers see "eye to eye." On the matter of race and ethnicity, yes, they have prominent places in my conception of imperialism, for the simple reason that the incidence of the exploitative effect of imperialism, as you know, fell more on some races than others. May I recall Aime Cesair[20] and the Caballero-Williams thesis on "the blackest thing in slavery."[21]

To say all this is not to be racist; far from it. To say this is to recognize the intended or the unintended, indeed, the necessary, racist and racialist accompaniment of the imperialist experience.[22]

I regard your reference to future history, formulating feasible and desirable future alternatives, as extremely important. To do this, we need to distinguish between future history as *celebration* of the past heroics and poetics from future history as the *invocation* of a preferred future.[23] All this is not easy to do, but I am convinced that a serious critique of Eurocentricity is unavoidable as the initial step in all this, given the nature of our given world.

Folker Fröbel: I would like to propose a modest scheme to represent my conception of "Eurocentricity." I solicit your reaction to my scheme; and I shall have to use the blackboard.

The following scheme is designed to exhibit a fundamental structure feature of the capitalist world-system (this world-system was the outcome/solution of the crisis of Western European feudalism).

World-System	Dominated by capitalist mode of production		Forms of exploitation of labour by capital	Forms of reproduction of labour (some examples)
Capitalism	Capital Labour	Internal proletariat:	Wage labour	Nuclear proletarian family
		External labour: (reproduction cost as far as capital has to for it in form of wages, etc.] is reduced in comparison with the case of the internal proletariat where increases in reproduction cost of labour are frequently constitutive of the model of accumulation)	Slavery Serfdom Simple commodity production (peasants, "informal sector," etc.) Immigrant labour (in industrial countries) Wage labour ("formal sector") Contract labour (e.g., in socialist countries)	Extraction from Africa Import from abroad

FIG. 3. Capitalcentricity of the world-system

In a Eurocentric interpretation of capitalism, only the elements within the inner box are *constitutive* elements in the analytic framework (= capitalcentric interpretation). The other elements (external labour, forms of reproduction of labour) are only *alluded to* in a *descriptive, ad hoc* manner or are totally neglected.

My point is that for the purposes of defining "Eurocentricity," the essence of capitalism is included only in the full scheme (including external labour, forms of reproduction of labour).

Addo: I agree with you; and, in particular, I like the term capitalcentric. I wish I had thought of it. I concede the idea is a good one, and so, even though it is not mine, I subscribe to it. It expresses a lot. I accept the exposition. It is elegant and very detailed. It is instructive. I think the two schemes are very compatible, in fact, complementary.

Fröbel: This is all very well, but is your way all the same not too exclusive of certain vital dimensions of the problem in hand? In fact, would you not say that your critique of Eurocentricity is part of a larger area for criticism, what I refer to as "capitalcentric," making a fetish of capital as Europeans wanted to understand it?

161

Addo: Yes, I would. Provided we agree that mine is an unfinished critique, which, by its unfinished mode, indicates other larger things like capitalcentricity.

Otto Kreye: In connection with your response to Folker's scheme, let me add what appears to me to be a vital aspect which seems missing in your treatment of the Eurocentric charge. There does not appear to be a discussion on the forms of exploitation which includes the forms of struggle against capitalist exploitation. Your exclusion of the labour movement — internal, external, and the contacts between them — is another dimension of Eurocentricity, don't you think? I think you should expand your scheme to include the dimensions you exclude but are included in Folker's scheme.

Addo: I suppose once a Eurocentric always a Eurocentric. You are perfectly right to point to these exclusions. At the moment, I am inclined to view my treatment of the Eurocentric charge as no more than introductory. The time will soon come when the treatment of the subject will have to be both deepened and broadened. When the time comes for the full elaboration of the Eurocentric indictment, be assured that I shall include your point which relates to Helen McEachrane's and Neville Duncan's, and can be placed under Folker Fröbel's. I shall expand the area of criticism. At the moment, I can appreciate these comments, but I think you will agree that I need time to reflect on them, if I am going to develop this line of thought further.

My thoughts, as they have developed to date, rather lack the quality of optimism. This much I admit. This is something that Samir Amin pointed out to me a couple of years ago, that Andre Gunder Frank also told me last year, and that Terence Hopkins spotted in a long discussion we had in Starnberg last summer.

My problem in this regard is not so much one of lack of optimism as one of a convincing lack of sources on which to hinge or rather anchor my transformational optimism. Very often when we refer to the "struggle," a term that is rapidly running into transformational ineffectiveness, we refer not to anti-systemic forces in the transformationally transitional sense but to the "musical chair" sense of anti-régime struggle. I have to be very careful here, for the strand separating the two can be very thin. But I have in mind here the extremely fruitful discussions we have had in the many colloquia at the Max-Planck-Institut between 1978 and 1980. I refer in particular to Frank's paper on Kampuchea,[24] Wallerstein's on anti-systemic forces,[25] to Ramkrishna Murkejee's oral intervention in the discussion on "crisis" at the 1980 colloquium.

I have in mind here what I have termed elsewhere as the distinction between valid and arrested transition potential.[26] My essential point is that I worry and wonder whether class struggle is not itself transformationally important, but, when carried to the focally fetish extreme, does not itself become a transitional hindrance in some circumstances where race, ethnicity, regionalism, even humanism must count much more.

To my mind, the main issue will always be the extent to which Eurocentricity as the dominant ideology downplays these other potentially valid transitional avenues and perspectives.

Galtung: This relates to your response to Kimon Valaskakis. I disagree very much with a visage of "imperialism" that divests the Roman Empire of it. I think that more than 1,000, in a sense, more than 2,000, years of Roman Empire history should weigh heavier than 50 to 100 years of Leninism with its conception of imperialism as the highest stage of capitalism, if by imperialism, we mean something like a division, geographically, into "internal" and "external" sectors with the former preying on the latter. Roman imperialism, with bridgeheads scattered around, cannot be excluded. What the Roman Empire was doing was mainly taxation and robbery. Therefore, while it was certainly not capitalist imperialism, it was certainly imperialism.

Imperialism can be of many types. Capitalist imperialism is more unambiguous. One can have either without the other and one can have the other followed by the other. The category of "capitalist imperialism" is different from "social imperialism," as Lin Biao termed it.

Addo: I was expecting this particular intervention from you. I welcome it. Allow me to respond to you, as my friend and teacher, in a combative way, aware as I am that you are the celebrated author of "A Structural Theory of Imperialism,"[27] the co-author of that provocative piece on the decline of the Roman Empire,[28] and very recently the author of "Imperialism: Twenty Years After."[29] I have learnt a lot from these works and many others by you, as you know.[30]

Galtung: I am happy you have found your combative self. I was thinking you were agreeing much too readily to too many things, very uncharacteristic from what I know about you.

Duncan: I think I know why Herb is agreeing so readily to things against which normally he would have argued combatively. As the chairman, I am in a position to tell you that it has been four hours now and I have just been told that lunch is almost, not almost but, in fact, ready.

Addo: I welcome the news on lunch. Four hours is by any reckoning too long to endure the searchlight you have focused on my position. I can do with a liquid break before lunch, though.

Duncan: Can't we all?

Addo: I guess we all can. I shall be brief, then, but I was going to say that I am familiar enough with Johan Galtung's works, some of them, at least, for he has written and spoken so much, to say that I know where the concerns for his last intervention originate.[31] However, I object to the 50 to 100 years Leninist conception of imperialism, as I have tried to make clear in the relevant chapter. At the same time, I wonder very much whether an imprecise 1,000 to 2,000 years' historical duration is necessarily an improvement and therefore better.

There are many similarities in form between the two imperialisms, but I submit that there are differences, too. In my scheme of thought, the differences are more important than any similarities between the two. I can easily agree with you that Roman imperialism was certainly an exploitation form, but can we agree that it was not capitalist and therefore different in vital historic terms? I am trying to distinguish capitalist imperialism in its unambiguous historic form from its other trans-historic kindred forms. Sure, one "imperialism" can be, in fact, is always, followed by other forms. My argument is simply that these different forms are not the same and, to the extent that they are not, precision demands that we recognize this for what it may be worth for the purpose of devising currently feasible transformational strategies.

Healey: I would like to refer to Folker's scheme. To the extent that it has anything to do with Herb's at all, Herb's includes Folker's. If Folker insists it can, then even when Folker does, it can still be argued that the entire "big box" is still Eurocentric even when related to the "small box."

164

Fröbel: The point I would like to get across is that one always needs terms of reference — criteria of appropriateness. One always needs a coherent set of explanatory values. One should always avoid voluntaristic explanations. Must one always relate goals to history in the form of a presentation in order to arrive at strategies?

Addo: I think Patrick Healey and Folker Fröbel should sort this out and let me know what they have agreed upon. I would like to know. I mean this.

Galtung: With respect to Folker Fröbel's position, I agree with Patrick's position that, to the extent it has anything to do with Addo's position at all, Addo's position includes it. However, since Folker has given his interpretation of Eurocentricity, permit me to give mine also: cosmology enters as a construction of the world that defines certain phenomena as more real than others. This disseminates through structures and systems of ideas, the accidents of cosmology, and a people see reality more or less the same way.

Addo: On this matter, I will only say that, while we cannot ignore the "genetic" imprints of cosmology and eschatology, to have full use for these fundamental historical bases, we need to have avenues for explaining to us why certain parts of the world became what they are, in contrast to what they are not, or no more, and how this relates to what they *are*, or *are not becoming*, or *never will*. I doubt very much if we can do all this without confronting Eurocentric epistemology four-squarely and critically with transformational sensibilities.

Duncan: Ladies and Gentlemen! Thank you for your participation. I am sure Herb thanks you for tasking him all morning.

Addo: Yes, I do very much, even though, as I have said, in the words of Walter Rodney, in these matters, responsibility is unavoidably collective. Mr. Chairman, may I say that I have been convinced by this long discussion that it will be wise for me to divide the manuscript discussed today into two volumes. This will call for many additions to make the second volume complete, but such additions will be the result of the inspirations and ideas I have obtained here this morning. Thank you all very much.

Duncan: I am glad to hear this. But what will you call these volumes?

Aseniero: That should be the least of his problems, as I see it.

Duncan: I agree. Thank you again. Lunch is served.

Notes

1. A fuller expression of this view can be found in my "African Political Institutions: Their Cultural Bases and Future Prospects," *Praxis International* 2, no. 2 (1982): 147–168.
2. Miklos Molnar, *Marx, Engels et La Politique Internationale* (Gallimard, Paris, 1975).
3. Johan Galtung, *Essays in Methodology; Methodology and Ideology: Theory and Method of Social Research*, vol. 1; *Papers on Methodology*, vol. 2 (Christian Ejlers, Copenhagen, 1979).
4. Immanuel Wallerstein, *The Modern World-System: Capitalist Agriculture and the Origins of the European World Economy in the Sixteenth Century* (Academic Press, New York, 1974).
5. Max Weber, *The Protestant Ethic and the Spirit of Capitalism* (Allen and Unwin, London, 1965).
6. "Histroid" was a term used in one of my papers presented at this meeting to describe a set of values constructed from the experiences, real or imagined, of the past which are to serve as the guide to a preferred future. The paper was titled "From History to 'Histroid': Looking Back to Look Forward" (Mimeo, 1980). The reader is referred to Herbert Marcuse, *Eros and Civilization* (Beacon Press, Boston, 1966), p. 19, where he writes, "... the orientation on the past trends toward an orientation on the future. The *recherche du temps perdu* becomes the vehicle of future liberation."
7. See my "Notes on the Making of a Third World Social Scientist in the Capitalist World," in Erik Rudeng and Hans-Henrik Holm, eds., *Social Science for What? A Festschrift in Honour of Johan Galtung* (Christian Ejlers, Copenhagen, 1980), pp. 31–36.
8. See the prologue.
9. I am referring to Herb Addo, ed. *Transforming the World-Economy? Nine Critical Essays on the New International Economic Order* (Hodder and Stoughton, London, 1984).
10. The reader is referred to the introduction and chapters one and two of Herb Addo et al., *Development as Social Transformation: Reflections on the Global Problematique* (Hodder and Stoughton, London, 1985).
11. See my chapter in the above volume and also my "Foreign Policy Strategies for Achieving the NIEO: A Third World Perspective," in Charles Kegley, Jr., and Patrick McGowan, eds., *The Political Economy of Foreign Policy Behaviour*, vol. 6 of *Sage Yearbook of Foreign Policy Studies* (Sage Publications, London, 1981), pp. 233–253.
12. See the references in note 10 above as well as my "Multiplicity of Images of Development in the Single Transformation of the World-System" (Mimeo, 1982).
13. I have subsequently expressed my disenchantment in the introductory pages of my contribution "Beyond Eurocentricity: Transformation and Transformational Responsibility," in Herb Addo et al., *Development as Social Transformation* (see note 10 above).
14. Andre Gorz, ed., *The Division of Labour: The Labour Process and Class Struggle in Modern Capitalism* (Humanities Press, Atlantic Highlands, N.J., 1976).
15. Reference is to McEachrane's intervention.

16. These thoughts can be found in my "Toward the Study of International Development: A Proposal," in *Caribbean Yearbook of International Relations* 2 (Sijthoff, The Hague, 1976), pp. 465–489.

17. Recall my response to Aseniero.

18. See Arghiri Emmanuel, *Unequal Exchange* (Monthly Review Press, New York, 1972), pp. 271–386.

19. See Ian Roxborough, *Theories of Underdevelopment* (Humanities Press, Atlantic Highlands, N.J., 1979), p. 62, and also my "Beyond Eurocentricity" (note 13 above).

20. I had in mind at this point the following quotation from Aime Cesaire, *Return to My Native Land* (Penguin Books, Harmondsworth, 1969), p. 17: "The peculiarity of 'our place in the world' which isn't to be confused with anybody else's. The peculiarity of our problems which aren't to be reduced to subordinate forms of any other problem. The peculiarity of our history, laced with terrible misfortunes which belong to no other history. The peculiarity of our culture, which we intend to live and to make live in an ever more real manner."

21. See Eric Williams, "The Blackest Thing in Slavery Was Not the Blackman," *Revisita InterAmericana* 3, no. 1 (1973): 1–23.

22. Since this was said, I have come across Rod Bush's article, "Racism and the Rise of the Right," *Contemporary Marxism* 4 (1982). See comments and responses to this article in no. 5 of the same journal, 154–158.

23. For further development of this distinction, see my "African Political Institutions: Their Cultural Bases and Future Prospects," *International Praxis* 2, no. 2: 148–167.

24. Andre Gunder Frank, "Kampuchea, Viet Nam, China: Observations and Reflections" (Research paper, United Nations University, Tokyo, 1982).

25. Immanuel Wallerstein, "Nationalism and the World Transition to Socialism: Is There a Crisis?" (Mimeo, 1980).

26. See references in notes 9 and 10 above.

27. Johan Galtung, "A Structural Theory of Imperialism," *Journal of Peace Research* 8, no. 1 (1971): 167–191.

28. Johan Galtung, Tore Heiestad, and Eric Ruge, "On the Decline and Fall of Empires: The Roman Empire and Western Imperialism Compared" (Research paper, United Nations University, Tokyo, 1979).

29. Johan Galtung, "Imperialism: Twenty Years After" (Mimeo, lecture delivered at London School of Economics, February 1981).

30. See my "Trends and Patterns in African Participation in International Relations, 1960–1970: Toward a Theory of International Development" (Unpublished Doctoral Thesis, Department of Political Science, Carleton University, Ottawa, Ontario, 1974).

31. I am referring to the citation in note 25 above.

Chapter Nine

Epilogue

Alexander Solzhenitsyn said something profound in his novel, *The First Circle*, to the effect that "a [person] won today is an embarrassment tomorrow."[1] In a similar vein, theorizations of today are usually embarrassments of tomorrow, because of the fact that none of them can ever claim to be fully complete; and usually their very incompleteness leads to more theorizations and more refinements.

Reflections on the contents of this book suggest to me that there is a need to deepen and widen the arguments which serve as the point of entry into the reality problem of the persistence of underdevelopment. I readily admit that I have done no more than scratch the surface of the problem. I only hope that, limitations and other embarrassments notwithstanding, the nature of the arguments is such that they invite us to scratch further, deeper, and wider, to reveal the real causes of the persistence and the permanence of imperialism.

If the initial worry was why imperialism persists, then further reflection suggests that, perhaps, the following question is in order: whether European social philosophy, liberal, radical, and Marxist, deliberately or not, has not simplified the explanation of the plight of the third world to mean the absence of European culture in these areas in order to propose the complicated answer of the imitation of the European ways of life through the imitation of European history by the third world societies as the solution.

If, in the final analysis, this is the question, then the suggestion still remains that relevant concepts should relate to the concept of *development* in such a way that the very axiology of the term development would imply by itself "what is to be done to develop." This will imply recognition of the dialectical unity of the centre and the periphery parts of the capitalist world. It will demand refinements in the meanings of such crucial concepts in the historico-processual sense within their capitalist historicity, in order to remove their current meanings from the dead and oppressive hands of the Eurocentric interpretation of human history and human future. The argument is that we should try to understand key concepts and the relationships between concepts within their own world-systemic context and not in the context of the European peculiarity within this world context.

This is all very well, but it still leaves us dealing with the *morphology* and the structure of the phenomenon and not its physiology, even within the world-system methodology.[2] The potential exists, however, in this methodology for us to approach the *physiology* of imperialism within the unicity of the world, from the value perspective of its transformation into a non-exploitative system.

To do this, we must not only begin by seeing the imperialist phenomenon as a complex property of the world-system, but we must also endeavour to reduce the complexity to a comprehensible simplicity which can serve as a genuine guide to efforts at transforming the world-system. One way of doing this is to reformulate the initial concern to ask *why* imperialism persists in the changing circumstances of the world-system.[3] Precisely, it is to ask why the societies of the periphery continue to act in such a manner as to make imperialism persistent, even at this post-independence phase of world-history.

The suggestion here is that to pursue this concern properly, we must see it, at one and the same time, as a complex set of "problems within problems," "issues within issues," "processes within processes," "paradoxes within paradoxes," and "negations within negations." We should then resolve the problems, issues, processes, paradoxes, and negations into a totalizing mode. This mode will express the fundamental contradiction in the imperialist phenomenon. This is the contradiction I shall call the *imperialist problématique* and which I shall describe as the (vexing) persistence of the exploitation nexus between the internal-periphery and the internal-centre sources of imperialism that operate to make imperialism both persistent and continuous, from the very beginning of world-history, in the late fifteenth century, until now.[4]

The imperialist problématique suggests a cardinal contradiction in the transformation of the world-system, the contradiction whereby things appear to change in the world context and yet remain essentially the same for the third world. Cardoso, for example, sees this matter in terms of how "... the same thing is *transformed* into the *other* by means of a

169

process which takes place in time and which brings certain classes into relation with others through struggle and opposes them to rival bloc...." (Emphases added.)[5] My question is: How *different* is the other? The main contradiction, to my mind, is exactly the paradoxical situation where the *other* remains essentially the same in the midst of apparent changes. The sameness in this instance is the reproduction of the historical processes within the capitalist historicity that lead to the enriching of the centre and the impoverishing of the periphery in various ways, expressing the historic constancy of the exploitation effects of imperialism on the periphery.

Further efforts in this direction must aim at showing that the viable points for negating the imperialist problématique include the internal-periphery end of it. Specifically, I shall be arguing that the politics of world-system transformation suggest that it is composed of a dialectical struggle between what I shall call *valid transition processes* and *arrested transition processes;*[6] and that since the periphery societies should be the main carriers of the valid transition processes, their internal orders are of crucial transformational importance.

If we accept that what has happened to post-independence expectations in the periphery of the world-system was not at all unusual, then in seeking to answer why this had to be so, we must realize at the outset that we are involved in the interpretation of history, the history of the capitalist world-system from its very beginning to its present post-independence phase. In interpreting a particular history for a particular purpose, two fundamental precepts must be obeyed.

The first is that the historicity, that is, the historic identity, of that epoch in human history must be respected. This is what we have insisted upon all along in this book: that the events constituting that history must be set in their *precise*, in their *immediate*, and in their *relevant* historical periodicity, if the difficult business of final causes is not to be carried to its absurd infinity or its absurd truncation. The meaning of the concept history itself connotes these conditions. To ignore these conditions is, as we have argued, to be either *imprecise* or *over-precise* in the presentation of a history. This means that one's presentation will tend to indulge in false comparison between falsely similar or falsely dissimilar historical events. In other words, one's presentation of history will tend to ignore the essential continuities and similarities between the same basic historical phenomenon or it will tend to establish false similarities between different historical phenomena.

The second fundamental precept is that to *interpret* history is to bring to bear on certain uncontested historical events a meaning which can be considered different from that usually held or originally intended. But the meaning of a particular history does not lie in itself. It lies in the meanings and in the significance we endow the concepts describing that history and in the interrelationships we establish between the meanings and the significance of these concepts. This means that the meaning of a particular history is contextually bound by the meanings and the significance of its descriptive and analytic concepts, in short, and to repeat, in its theory. It is these two precepts which make history and theory in political economy the same thing, as Frank argues.[7]

In political economy, one ideology will always exist in competition with other ideologies, but this is not an interesting point. The interesting point is that to interpret history for one partisan purpose or the other, key historical concepts will have to be reinterpreted and/or used in new interrelationships to provide a new theory. It is worth recalling, in this context, Wallerstein's argument that, for living men, the important thing is to situate the options available in their contemporary situation in terms of the patterns they can discern in the historical past; and that in this task, "conceptual clarification is the most constant need, and as life goes on and new experiences occur, we learn, if we are wise, to reject and reformulate the partial truths of our predecessors, and to unmask the ideological obscurantism of the self-interested upholders of encrusted privilege."[8]

These are profound words, which Cedric Robinson concurs with. He states: "... I believe the most important issue is conceptualization."[9] Robinson used these words in an essay on the third world and the dialectic of imperialism, an essay he began by asking the following important question: "How are we to conceptualize what we were, what we are, what we are becoming?"[10]

Robinson's task, for which these questions served well, "was to achieve a means of conceptualizing change, specifically the developments among black peoples which constituted their response to the incorporation of their labour and lives into the emerging system of world capitalism in the nineteenth century."[11] The future task, as I see it now and for which these same questions may also serve well, is to conceptualize the other side of the dialectic: the lack of change in the historic meaning of the *common* lot of third world societies in world-history. The main question, therefore, is this: What have these societies not become and why?

171

By referring to the common lot of third world societies in world-history, I am not saying that the third world is a homogeneous unit, a monolith. There are differences between the separate societies within the third world, brought about by the distinctiveness of their individual histories within world-history. This is not, and never can be, the point of contention. What is bothersome and contentious is the tendency among some dependency theorists to consider it part of their method to decry any historic commonality attributed to the third world as such, or parts of it.[12]

The historic commonality I am referring to is the continuity of the exploitation of these parts of the world-system by the centre, all through world-history. The degree and the mode of exploitation may differ from place to place within the periphery, but this hardly detracts from the commonality of persisting exploitation resulting in the institutionalized inabilities to accumulate capital within peripheral societies. When I come to address this matter, I shall argue that to ignore exploitation as the common characteristic identity of the historic lot of third world countries is to fall in a most injudicious trap, the intellectual equivalent of the imperialist political tactic of divide and rule.

A general depiction of the peripheral commonality, *the plight*, is no substitute for the detailed study of the societal specifics within the periphery, but, then, it is without prejudice to the study of these specifics either. The two must go hand in hand in that it is from the commonality of the peripheral plight that we can deduce other peripheral generalities, including the apparently different, but essentially similar, attempts to imitate the different forms that the European ways of life take. All this, to reiterate, is without prejudice to the peculiar specifics of individual societies.

The undertaking to investigate history inevitably reveals that it is futile to condemn, blame, or even censure history of the past; and that those who find much to be pleased about in past history will tend to value it as a matter of, and for, *celebration*. Such people will tend to appreciate past history in terms of the past poetics and the past heroics which they would like to see more or less emulated at a particular time and extrapolated into a particular future. In this conception of *history as celebration*, the present, as it mediates between the past and the future, is evaluated in terms of its departures from and its insufficiencies in the glorified past.

Those who do not find much to be pleased about in a particular past history tend to place more emphasis on preferred future history, basing this preferred history on the few redeeming aspects of past history. This is the conception of *history as invocation.* And in this conception of history, the present, as it mediates between the past and the preferred future, is invariably found wanting in the few redeeming aspects of past history. It is for this reason that the conception of history as invocation has that slight touch of *the prophetic.* This conception of history tends to warn about dire consequences for future history which will issue from the non-retrieval and the non-application of the few basic redeeming factors in past history.

I take the invocatory view of future history; and by so doing, I am not suggesting that the peoples of the periphery have not endured a lot nor that they have not contributed a lot to world-history, in the celebratory sense; far from it. They have, and this is clearly demonstrated in many history books. What I am suggesting deals with the dialectical counterpart of this historical fact as it applies in contemporary history, the immediate parent of future history: the vital need to confront domination with subordination.

My essential argument is that, from a transformational perspective, the roles of the peripheral state in contemporary history give cause not for *celebratory abandon* but for *solemn invocation.* This fact is crucial for any further study of the subject. From my perspective within the world-system methodology, I shall argue that, if there is very little to celebrate transformationally in world-history, as it stands at its contemporary phase, there is even less to celebrate, in the transformational sense, in the role that the peripheral state, and specifically the peripheral intellectual component within it, plays at this present phase of world-history.[13]

That is why I approach history as a matter of preferred future. That is to say, I approach history as a matter of transformed future, as a matter of preferred transformation, and hence as a matter of a much-needed invocation. May I add that prophecy may have a lot to do with invocation, but the two are not identical. Invocation, insofar as it has to do with prophecy, differs from a well-founded prediction, but only to the extent that one ignores or undervalues the arguments upon which the invocation is based.[14]

For these reasons, I should endeavour to understand history in a manner which will enable me to invoke its future form along some preferred lines. In doing this, I should not pretend to write history. I should only attempt to use my understanding of it to invoke the future.

I am very much aware that, by adopting the invocatory approach to history to treat the role of the peripheral society in transforming the world, I open myself to all kinds of criticisms from an established orthodoxy in which concepts, theories, and derivative questions concerning the emergence of the peripheral state, the role of the state itself, and the role of the intellectuals within it all relate to the appreciation of history as a cause for celebration. I am aware of this; and I expect that some of the criticisms, received and anticipated, will be valid.

I must be frank and fair by saying that, if some readers criticize this work and its sequel not along the lines and in the spirit in which it is written, and is meant to be read and appreciated, but along the lines that they themselves would have written the book, I cannot help it. My remembrances make it so. What I can say is that this habit comes with a huge risk. It prolongs the reproductions of the variations in the same basic Eurocentric dominant themes in political economy. This is not meant to evade or to stop criticism. It is meant to force it to break its standard Eurocentric bounds.

My argument at this point is that this book and its follow-ups may even be frankly naïve and a disappointment. But it should be noted that its reasoning attempts to defy the persisting worship at the eternal shrine of "the complexity of the problem" and unreflected references to begging the question because the question may be incomprehensible to dominant methodology. I would like to think that the overall provocative flavour of this book defies glib references to simplistic, even benign, fascination with notions of the continuing adaptation-survival and, in particular, the demise of the peripheral state, and with this, the demise of the constructive roles that the intellectuals of the periphery can play in transforming the world for the better, once they (we) come to understand their roles in this regard. In particular, the provocation is directed against the dangerous notion that philosophers have contemplated the world long enough and that all we need do is to go out there and change it. This belief is dangerous because the *preferred*, the *dominant*, and the *serious* contemplations that have been done of the modern world-system are

174

those of the Eurocentric kind; and, as a result, the dominant prescriptions as to how to change it are, necessarily, Eurocentric.

The most glaring problem in political economy today is the situation where orthodoxy encourages programmed late twentieth century personalities to use nineteenth century thought forms to tackle twenty-first century problems.[15] This is sad all round, but it is even sadder in the case of third world scholarship, to the development of which I am committed, when we realize that from the peripheral point of view within the world-system methodology, what we should begin to know about the transformational problem is that it is a twenty-first century problem in search of twenty-first century personalities, equipped with twenty-first century thought forms.

In the final analysis, then, what is really involved in our intellectual and practical searches for developmental alternatives is the necessity to move from the prevailing Eurocentric cultural concept of the idea of development to historical concepts of different cultural ideas of development.[16]

Notes

1. Alexander Solzhenitsyn, *The First Circle* (Bantam Books, New York, 1976).
2. I am grateful to Ramkrisha Murkherjee of the Centre for Appraisal of Social Reality and Quality of Life, Calcutta, for making this point exceedingly clear to me in lengthy correspondence. See his *What Will It Be? Explorations in Inductive Sociology* (Carolina Academic Press, Durham, N.C., 1978).
3. This is the main question addressed in my "Beyond Eurocentricity: Transformation and Transformational Responsibility," in Herb Addo et al., *Development as Social Transformation: Reflections on the Global Problematique* (Hodder and Stoughton, London, 1985). The idea is to develop it fully in volume two.
4. For the initial ideas on this, see chapter nine of Herb Addo, ed., *Transforming the World-Economy? Nine Critical Essays on the New International Economic Order* (Hodder and Stoughton, London, 1984).
5. Fernando Henrique Cardoso, "The Consumption of Dependency Theory in the United States," *Latin American Research Review* 7, no. 3 (1977): 16.
6. For a discussion of these processes, see chapter nine of *Transforming the World-Economy?* (note 4 above).
7. Andre Gunder Frank, *World Accumulation, 1492–1789* (Macmillan, London, 1978), p. 13.
8. Immanuel Wallerstein, in H. Muñoz, ed., *From Dependency to Development: Strategies to Overcome Underdevelopment and Inequality* (Westview Press, Boulder, Col., 1981), p. 268.
9. Cedric Robinson, "Coming to Terms: The Third World and the Dialectic of Imperialism," *Race and Class* 22, no. 4 (1981): 263.
10. Robinson (see note 9 above), p. 263.

11. Robinson (see note 9 above), p. 263.
12. Many references can be cited in support of this claim. They include: J. Samuel Valenzuela and Arturo Valenzuela, "Modernization and Dependency: Alternative Perspectives in the Study of Latin American Development," pp. 15–41, James A. Caporaso and Behrouz Zare, "An Interpretation and Evaluation of Dependency Theory," pp. 43–56, Fernando Henrique Cardoso, "Towards Another Development," pp. 295–313, in H. Muñoz, ed., *From Dependency to Development* (see note 8 above); Ian Roxborough, *Theories of Underdevelopment* (Humanities Press, Atlantic Highlands, N.J., 1979); Peter Evans, *Dependent Development: The Alliance of Multi-national, State, and Local Capital in Brazil* (Princeton University Press, Princeton, N.J., 1979); Fernando Henrique Cardoso and Enzo Faletto, *Dependency and Development in Latin America* (University of California Press, Berkeley, Calif., 1979); Fernando Henrique Cardoso, "The Consumption of Dependency Theory in the United States," *Latin American Research Review* 12, no. 3 (1977): 7–24; James A. Caporaso, "Dependence, Dependency, and Power in the Global System: A Structural and Behavioral Analysis," *International Organization* 32, no. 1 (1978): 13–43; and David A. Baldwin, "Interdependence and Power: A Conceptual Analysis," *International Organization* 34, no. 4 (1980): 471–506.
13. On this matter of intellectual component, see some initial thoughts in my "Beyond Eurocentricity" (note 3 above), pp. 40–42.
14. The reader is referred to Walter Kaufmann's treatment of "Prophecy," Jewish prophecy, to be exact, in Martin Buber, *I and Thou* (Charles Scribner's Sons, New York, 1970), p. 29.
15. This is a paraphrase of William Simon's statement that much of his conclusion "... can be readily observed in many current elections where 17th–18th century personalities utilizing 20th century communication systems contest for control of a 19th century political system that will make decisions regarding the 21st century." From William Simon, "Cultural Demography of a Society in Transition," in Magda Cordell- McHale, ed., *Expanding the Horizons of Our Arts: Proceedings of the Biannual Conference of the Theatre Communication Group*, New York, 1980 (forthcoming, Pergamon Press).
16. See my "Crisis in the Development Praxis: A Critical Global Perspective" (Mimeo, 1984), for some initial extensions of this matter.

Select Bibliography

Addo, H. "Toward the Study of International Development: A Proposal." In *Caribbean Yearbook of International Relations* 2, 465–489. Sijthoff, The Hague, 1976.

———. "The New International Economic Order and Imperialism: A Context for Evaluation." *IPRA Studies in Peace Research, Proceedings of the Seventh IPRA Conference* 7 (1979): 194–215.

———. "Foreign Policy Strategies for Achieving the New International Economic Order: A Third World Perspective." In C. Kegley and P. McGowan, eds., *The Political Economy of Foreign Policy Behavior*, 233–253. Vol. 6 of *Sage Yearbook of Foreign Policy Studies*. Sage Publications, London, 1980.

———. "Approaching the New International Economic Order Dialectically and Transformationally." Research paper, United Nations University, Tokyo, 1982.

———. "Prologue: The Eurocentric State of the Discipline." Research paper, United Nations University, Tokyo, 1982.

———. "African Political Institutions: Their Cultural Bases and Future Prospects." *International Praxis* 2, no. 2 (1982): 148–167.

———. "Multiplicity of Images of Development in the Single Transformation of the World-System." Mimeo, 1982.

———, ed. *Transforming the World-Economy? Nine Critical Essays on the New International Economic Order*. Hodder and Stoughton, London, 1984.

———. "Crisis in the Development Praxis: A Critical Global Perspective." Mimeo, 1984.

———, et al. *Development as Social Transformation: Reflections on the Global Problematique*. Hodder and Stoughton, London, 1985.

Amin, S. *Accumulation on a World-Scale: A Critique of the Theory of Underdevelopment*. 2 vols. Monthly Review Press, New York, 1974.

———. "The Early Roots of Unequal Exchange." *Monthly Review* 27, no. 7 (1975): 43–47.

———. *Unequal Development: An Essay on the Social Formations of Peripheral Capitalism*. Harvester Press, Sussex, 1976.

———. *Imperialism and Unequal Development*. Monthly Review Press, New York, 1977.

———. *Class and Nations, Historically and in the Current Crisis*. Monthly Review Press, London, 1980.

Arendt, H. *Imperialism: The Origins of Totalitarianism*. Allen and Unwin, London, 1968.

Arrighi, G. *The Geometry of Imperialism: The Limits of Hobson's Paradigm*. NLB, London, 1978.

Aseniero, G. "A Reflection on Developmentalism: From Development to Transformation." Chap. 2 in H. Addo et al., *Development as Social Transformation*.

Bagchi, A.K. "A Note on the Requirements of a Theory of Imperialism." Mimeo, 1980.

Baldwin, D.A. "Inter-dependence and Power: A Conceptual Analysis." *International Organization* 34, no. 4 (1980): 471–506.

Baran, P.A. *The Political Economy of Growth.* Modern Reader Paperbacks, New York, 1968.

Baran, P.A., and P.M. Sweezy. *Monopoly Capital: An Essay on the American Economic and Social Order.* Monthly Review Press, New York, 1966.

——. "Notes on the Theory of Imperialism." In K.T. Fann and D.C. Hodges, eds., *Readings in US Imperialism.*

Bauer, O. *Die Nationalitätenfrage und die Sozialdemokratie.* Marx-Studien, Vienna, 1907.

Boulding, K.E., and T. Mukerjee, eds. *Economic Imperialism.* University of Michigan Press, Ann Arbor, Mich., 1972.

Brenner, R. "The Origins of Capitalist Development: A Critique of Neo-Smithian Marxism." *New Left Review* 104 (1977): 25–93.

——. "Reply to Sweezy." *New Left Review* 108 (March–April 1978).

——. "Dobb on the Transition from Feudalism to Capitalism." *Cambridge Journal of Economics* 2 (1978): 121–140.

Brown, M.B. "A Critique of Marxist Theories of Imperialism." In R. Owen and B. Sutcliffe, eds., *Studies in the Theory of Imperialism.*

Bukharin, N. *Imperialism and World Economy.* Merlin Press, London, 1976.

Caporaso, J. "Dependence, Dependency, and Power in the Global System: A Structural and Behavioral Analysis." *International Organization* 32, no. 1 (1978): 13–43.

Caporaso, J., and B. Zare. "An Interpretation and Evaluation of Dependency Theory." In H. Muñoz, ed., *From Dependency in Development: Strategies to Overcome Underdevelopment and Inequality.*

Cardoso, F.H. "Dependency and Development in Latin America." *New Left Review* 74 (1972): 83–95.

——. "Towards Another Development." In H. Muñoz, ed., *From Dependency to Development: Strategies to Overcome Underdevelopment and Inequality.*

Cardoso, F.H., and E. Faletto. *Dependency and Development in Latin America.* University of California Press, Berkeley, Calif., 1979.

Casanova, P.G. "Historical Systems and Social Systems." *Studies in Comparative International Development* 8, no. 2 (1973): 227–246.

Chase-Dunn, C. "Comparative Research on World-System Characteristics." *International Studies Quarterly* 23, no. 4 (1979): 601–623.

Cohen, B.J. *The Question of Imperialism: The Political Economy of Dominance and Dependency.* Macmillan, London, 1974.

Cohen, R.B., et al., eds. *The Multinational Corporation: A Radical Approach, Papers by Stephen Herbert Hymer.* Cambridge University Press, London, 1979.

Cordell-McHale, M., ed. *Expanding the Horizons of Our Arts: Proceedings of the Biannual Conference of the Theatre Communication Group.* Pergamon, New York, 1980.

Cox, O.C. *Capitalism as a System.* Monthly Review Press, New York, 1964.

Dobb, M. *Studies in the Development of Capitalism.* Routledge and Kegan Paul, London, 1975.

Emmanuel, A. *Unequal Exchange: A Study of the Imperialism of Trade.* Monthly Review Press, New York, 1972.

——. "White-Settler Colonialism and the Myth of Investment Imperialism." *New Left Review* 73 (1973): 35–57.

——. "Myths of Development Versus Myths of Underdevelopment." *New Left Review* 85 (1974): 61–82.

——. "Gains and Losses from the International Division of Labour." *Review* 1, no. 2 (1977): 87–108.

Evans, P. *Dependent Development: The Alliance of Multinational, State, and Local Capital in Brazil.* Princeton University Press, Princeton, N.J., 1979.

Fann, K.T., and D.C. Hodges, eds. *Readings in US Imperialism.* Porter Sargent, Boston, Mass., 1971.

Fieldhouse, D.K. "Imperialism: A Historiographical Revision." In K.E. Boulding and T. Mukerjee, eds., *Economic Imperialism.*

Finley, M.I. "Empire in the Graeco-Roman World." *Review* 2, no. 1 (1978): 55–68.

Frank, A.G. *Latin America: Underdevelopment or Revolution.* Monthly Review Press, New York, 1969.

———. *Dependent Accumulation and Underdevelopment.* Macmillan, London, 1978.

———. *World Accumulation, 1492–1789.* Macmillan, London, 1978.

———. "Unequal Accumulation: Intermediate, Semi-Peripheral, and Sub-Imperialism Economies." *Review* 2, no. 3 (1979): 281–350.

———. *Crisis: In the Third World.* Holmes and Meier, New York, 1980.

———. *Crisis: In the World Economy.* Holmes and Meier, New York, 1980.

Friedman, J. "Crises in the Theory of Transformations of the World Economy." *Review* 2, no. 2 (1978): 131–146.

Fröbel, F. "The Current Development of the World Economy." Research paper, United Nations University, Tokyo, 1980.

Fröbel, F., J. Heinrichs, and O. Kreye. "The Tendency Towards a New International Division of Labor." *Review* 1, no. 1 (1977): 73–88.

———. "The New International Division of Labour." *Social Science Information* 17, no. 1 (1980): 123–142.

———. *The New International Division of Labour.* Cambridge University Press, Cambridge, 1981.

Gallagher, J., and R. Robinson. "Imperialism and Free Trade." *Economic History Review*, series 2, 6, no. 1 (1953).

Galtung, J. "A Structural Theory of Imperialism." *Journal of Peace Research* 8, no. 1 (1971): 167–191.

———. *Methodology and Ideology: Theory and Method of Social Research*, vol. 1. Christian Ejlers, Copenhagen, 1977.

———. "Global Goals, Global Processes and the Prospects for Human and Social Development." Mimeo, 1979.

———. "Imperialism: Twenty Years After." Mimeo, 1981.

Galtung, J., T. Heiestad, and E. Ruge. "On the Decline and Fall of Empires: The Roman Empire and Western Imperialism Compared." Research paper, United Nations University, Tokyo, 1978.

Gorz, A., ed. *The Division of Labour: The Labour Process and Class Struggle in Modern Capitalism.* Humanities Press, Atlantic Highlands, N.J., 1976.

Heilbroner, R.L. *The Future as History: The Historic Currents of Our Time and the Direction in Which They Are Taking America.* Grove Press, New York, 1961.

———. *The Future as History.* Harper and Row, New York, 1968.

———. *An Inquiry into the Human Prospect.* Calder and Boyars, London, 1975.

Hilferding, R. *Das Finanzkapital: Eine Studie über die jüngste Entwicklung des Kapitalismus.* Brand, Vienna, 1910.

Hilton, R. *The Transition from Feudalism to Capitalism.* New Left Books, London, 1976.

Hobsbawn, E.J. *The Age of Capital 1848–1875.* Weidenfeld and Nicolson, London, 1975.

Hobson, J.A. *Imperialism: A Study.* Allen and Unwin, London, 1951.

Hodgkin, T. "Some African and Third World Theories of Imperialism." In R. Owen and B. Sutcliffe, eds., *Studies in the Theory of Imperialism.*

Hopkins, T.K. "World-System Analysis: Methodological Issues." In B.H. Kaplan, ed., *Social Change in the Capitalist World Economy.*

Hopkins, T.K., and I. Wallerstein. "Patterns of Development of the Modern World-System: Research Proposal." *Review* 1, no. 2 (1977): 111–145.

Insurgent Sociologist, special issue on imperialism and the state, vol. 7, no. 2 (1977).

Kaplan. B.H., ed. *Social Change in the Capitalist World Economy*. Sage Publications, London, 1978.

Kautsky, K. "Ultra-Imperialism." *New Left Review* 59 (1970).

Kemp, T. "The Marxist Theory of Imperialism." In R. Owen and B. Sutcliffe, eds., *Studies in the Theory of Imperialism*.

Koebner, R. "The Concept of Economic Imperialism." In K.E. Boulding and T. Mukerjee, eds., *Economic Imperialism*.

Kreye, O. "Perspectives for Development through Industrialization in the 1980s: An Independent View on Dependency." Research paper, United Nations University, Tokyo, 1980.

Laclau, E. "Feudalism and Capitalism in Latin America." *New Left Review* 67 (1971).

——. *Politics and Ideology in Marxist Theory: Capitalism, Fascism, Populism.* Humanities Press, London, 1977.

Lall, S. "Is Dependence a Useful Concept in Analysing Underdevelopment?" *World Development* 3, nos. 11 and 12 (1975): 799–810.

Landes, D.S. "The Nature of Economic Imperialism." In K.E. Boulding and T. Mukerjee, eds., *Economic Imperialism*.

Lenin, V.I. *Imperialism: The Highest Stage of Capitalism*. International Publishers, New York, 1969.

Luxemburg, R. *The Accumulation of Capital*. Routledge and Kegan Paul, London, 1963.

McDonald, R. "The Williams Thesis: A Comment on the State of Scholarship." *Caribbean Quarterly* 25, no. 3 (1979): 63–68.

MacEwan, A. "Capitalist Expansion, Ideology and Intervention." *The Review of Radical Political Economics* 4, no. 1 (1972): 36–58.

McGowan, P. "Problems of Theory and Data in the Study of World-System Dynamics." Paper presented at the 21st Annual Convention of the International Studies Association, Los Angeles, 18–22 March, 1980.

Machlup, F. *Essays on Economic Semantics*. Prentice Hall, Englewood Cliffs, N.J., 1963.

Magdoff, H. *The Age of Imperialism*. Monthly Review Press, New York, 1969.

——. "How to Make a Molehill Out of a Mountain: Reply to Szymanski." *The Insurgent Sociologist* 7, no. 2 (1977): 106–112.

——. *Imperialism: From the Colonial Age to the Present*. Monthly Review Press, New York, 1978.

——. "Harry Magdoff Replies." *Monthly Review* 30 (May 1978): 57–61.

Malizia, E. "Imperialism Reconsidered; A Review of Arghiri Emmanuel, Unequal Exchange: A Study of the Imperialism of Trade." *The Review of Radical Political Economics* 5, no. 2 (1973): 87–92.

Molnar, M. *Marx, Engels et La Politique Internationale*. Gallimard, Paris, 1975.

Muñoz, H., ed. *From Dependency to Development: Strategies to Overcome Underdevelopment and Inequality*. Westview Press, Boulder, Col., 1981.

Nisbet, R.A. *Social Change and History: Aspects of the Western Theory of Development*. Oxford University Press, London, 1969.

Nkrumah, K. *Neo-Colonialism: The Last Stage of Imperialism*. Heinemann, Ibadan, 1968.

O'Connor, J. "The Meaning of Economic Imperialism." In K.T. Fann and D.C. Hodges, eds., *Readings in US Imperialism*.

Owen, R., and B. Sutcliffe, eds. *Studies in the Theory of Imperialism*. Longman, London, 1972.

Palma, G. "Dependency: A Formal Theory of Underdevelopment or a Methodology for the Analysis of Concrete Situations of Underdevelopment?" *World Development* 6 (1978): 881–924.

Review, special issue on cycles and trends, vol. 2, no. 4 (1979).

Richards, L. "The Context of Foreign Aid, Modern Imperialism." *The Review of Radical Political Economics* 4, no. 1 (1972): 53–58.

Robinson, C. "Coming to Terms: The Third World and the Dialectic of Imperialism." *Race and Class* 22, no. 4 (1981): 363–386.

Rosen, J.R., and R.K. James, eds. *Testing Theories of Economic Imperialism*. D.C. Heath, Lexington, Mass., 1974.

Roxborough, I. *Theories of Underdevelopment*. Macmillan, London, 1979.

Sau, R. *Unequal Exchange, Imperialism and Underdevelopment: Essays on Political Economy of World Capitalism*. Oxford University Press, New Delhi, 1978.

Schumpeter, J.A. *Imperialism and Social Classes*. Augustus M. Kelly, New York, 1951.

———. "On Imperialism." In K.E. Boulding and T. Mukerjee, eds., *Economic Imperialism*.

Simon, W. "Cultural Demography of a Society in Transition." In M. Cordell-McHale, ed., *Expanding the Horizons of Our Arts: Proceedings of the Biannual Conference of the Theatre Communication Group*.

Strachey, J. *The End of Empire*. Gollancz, London, 1959.

Sutcliffe, B. "Imperialism and Industrialization in the Third World." In R. Owen and B. Sutcliffe, eds., *Studies in the Theory of Imperialism*.

———. "Conclusion." In R. Owen and B. Sutcliffe, eds., *Studies in the Theory of Imperialism*.

Sweezy, P.M. *The Theory of Capitalist Development*. Monthly Review Press, New York, 1970.

———. "Marxian Economics." *Monthly Review* 28, no. 7 (1976): 1–6.

———. "Comment on Brenner." *New Left Review* 108 (March–April 1978).

Szymanski, A. "A Response to Andre Gunder Frank and Martin Murray." *The Review of Radical Political Economics* 8, no. 2 (1976): 77–83.

———. "Capital Accumulation on a World Scale and the Necessity of Imperialism." *The Insurgent Sociologist* 7, no. 2 (1977): 35–53.

———. "Even Mountains are Moved: A Response to Magdoff." *Monthly Review* 30 (May 1978): 48–57.

Valenzuela, J.S., and A. Valenzuela. "Modernization and Dependency: Alternative Perspectives in the Study of Latin American Development" In H. Muñoz, ed., *From Dependency to Development: Strategies to Overcome Underdevelopment and Inequality*.

Wallerstein, I. *The Modern World-System: Capitalist Agriculture and the Origins of the European World Economy in the Sixteenth Century*. Academic Press, New York, 1974.

———. "A World-System Perspective on the Social Sciences." *The British Journal of Sociology* 27, no. 3 (1976): 343–352.

———. "Imperialism and Development." Paper presented at the Marshall Woods Lecture, Brown University, 1977. In Albert Bergeson, ed., *Studies of the Modern World System*. Academic Press, New York, 1980.

———. "World-System Analysis: Theoretical and Interpretative Issues." In B.H. Kaplan, ed., *Social Change in the Capitalist World Economy*.

———. *The Capitalist World-Economy*. Cambridge University Press, Cambridge, 1979.

———. *The Modern World-System II: Mercantilism and the Consolidation of the European World-Economy, 1600–1750*. Academic Press, New York, 1980.

———. "Dependence in an Interdependent World: The Limited Possibilities of Transformation within the Capitalist World Economy." In H. Muñoz, ed., *From Dependency to Development: Strategies to Overcome Underdevelopment and Inequality*. Reprinted from *African Studies Review* 18, no. 1 (1974): 1–26.

Warren, B. "Imperialism and Capitalist Industrialization." *New Left Review* 81 (1973): 3–44.

———. *Imperialism, the Pioneer of Capitalism*. NLB, London, 1980.

Weisskopf, T. "Capitalism, Underdevelopment and the Future of the Poor Countries." *The Review of Radical Political Economics* 4, no. 1 (1972): 1–35.

——. "Theories of American Imperialism: A Critical Evaluation." *The Review of Radical Political Economics* 6, no. 3 (1974): 41–60.

Williams, E. *Capitalism and Slavery.* University of North Carolina Press, Chapel Hill, N.C., 1944.

——. *British Historians and the West Indies.* Andre Deutsch, London, 1966.

——. *From Columbus to Castro: The History of the Caribbean 1492–1969.* Andre Deutsch, London, 1978.

Winslow, E.M. *The Pattern of Imperialism: A Study in Theories of Power.* Octagon Press, New York, 1972.

Wolfe, R. "American Imperialism and the Peace Movements." In K.T. Fann and D.C. Hodges, eds., *Readings in US Imperialism.*